HOLY LOCKDOWN

Does the Church Limit Black Progress?

Jeremiah Camara

Twelfth House Publishing

Holy Lockdown
Does the Church Limit Black Progress?

ISBN: 0-9747967-0-0
Library of Congress Control Number: 2004092753
www.twelvehp.com

DEDICATIONS

Dedicated to all Lovers of Freedom, Advocators of Change, Embracers of Ideas, Respecters of Knowledge, Appreciators of Beauty, Admirers of Intelligence, and Users of Imagination.

Peace & Prosperity

Jeremiah Camara

Acknowledgements

I would like to thank my mother and father for loving me and always allowing me the freedom to express my ideas, no matter how eccentric they may have been. You never forced me to attend, become a member of a church, or be a part of any organized religion. You always gave me choices and allowed my imagination to reign free with access to infinity. I was never taught what to think, only how to think. Thank You. Eternal love and gratitude to you both.

Holy Lockdown

CONTENTS

Introduction

The social and psychological impact that the African American church has made on the psyche of Black people has been a concern for many years. When I initially considered writing a book that would challenge, question, and criticize the church, I began to feel as if I were a traitor to my people. Criticizing the church, in the eyes of most Blacks, has always been considered blasphemy and a forbidden thing to do. Black people have driven past the hardships of an oppressive American system mainly on the fuel provided by our churches. This great institution has been the pillar of strength bringing forth a doctrine of hope during slavery to the present. It is difficult to state my position in this book with complete candor, without being misconstrued, misunderstood, or accused of attacking the Almighty. Many people, perhaps a majority, will draw inaccurate conclusions about me. I may even be regarded by some as a lost soul who has not yet experienced the "true" spirit of God. This interpretation would be entirely false.

We are all entitled to our beliefs and opinions; however, my own personal gratification in writing a book of this nature lies in the sincerity of its content. Right, wrong, or in between, writing this book was something I felt compelled to do, despite the possibility of public backlash. I anticipate that the majority of those who read *Holy Lockdown* will claim their church and preacher are different and the accusations levied throughout this book do not directly apply to them. A common argument in defense of the church is that today's contemporary Black churches are different from those of the past, provide modern messages, and are more in step with the new generation. Maybe this is true to a certain extent, but the perceived differences are not distinctive enough to separate them from the long tradition of Black churches in America. In my opinion, if these claims of being different were true, then our communities and collective conditions would reflect such differences and we would see more fruit from the church's labor. This is especially reasonable since it seems as if there is a church on every corner in the Black community.

A new generation of African American preachers has emerged on the national and international scene. In our expanding world of Black clergy, they are the superstars.

These popular preachers are not necessarily disseminating new information but simply coloring the language of traditional sermonic rhetoric.

For the record, I am not an atheist, nor am I taking aim at any particular religion. I am simply demonstrating love. You are sometimes critical of those you love, and the love for my people gives me the courage to share with them what I feel is of importance. I strongly believe that affiliations with organized religions can sometimes be problematic when we form cliques with those who worship as we do. This creates theosophical wedges and contributes to our fragmentation. Driving greater wedges is the fact that there are many of us that do not have the slightest clue about the origin of our particular religion or belief system. Many are oblivious to the historical circumstances, motivation, and politics behind the establishment of our particular belief.

The irony of our various belief systems is that they are amongst our greatest dividers. It is rare, for instance, to see Blacks of different denominations collaborating in business ventures. Our variety of denominations is an example of many calculated divide and conquer strategies used against us in order to dismantle our cultural infrastructure. Adding to an already fragmented mix are the so-called non-denominational churches that exist within our communities. Belonging to a non-denominational church is like wearing generic clothing.

Although no name brand is attached to the clothing, it still looks very similar to the popular brands.

To criticize the church may seem like going against nature because the church has been the mainstay of our experience in America, and, for generations, the only institution consistently serving in the interest of Blacks.

In an attempt to assuage my doubts about confronting such a sensitive subject, I reminded myself that some of the most radical ideas and actions have amounted to some of the most enlightening achievements. I also knew that God and the church are not one in the same, and every fruit that grows from the tree of the church should not be eaten.

To address what I believe are negative aspects of the church, I had to first make sure that I was familiar with its inner-workings. There was a time in my life when I considered becoming a minister, or at least living an active life in the church. In my early twenties, living in Cleveland, Ohio, I attended a Baptist church at least two or three times a week. Although I was heavily influenced by jazz music as a child, the only music I listened to at that time was gospel. My new friends were deeply involved in the church and, for a brief time, I lived with a preacher. Ironically, as a child I was not raised in the church. My parents were not consistent churchgoers and never insisted that I or my brothers and sisters attend church. However, I did manage to go quite often.

During this particular searching period in Cleveland, I needed answers, meaning, and purpose in my life. Like many people, I felt the church could provide me with the substance my life was missing. There came a time, however, when I began to distance myself from the church, but not because of any particular bad experience or negative incident. It was because I was researching and exposing myself to other forms of thought, spiritual concepts and ideas. I began to see the church as just *one* source and not the only source of guidance and inspiration. The diversity of the world and its kaleidoscopic array of infinite wisdom and ideas would not permit my spirit to be confined only to the teachings of the church. It also disturbed me deeply to witness Blacks praising much but producing little. I asked myself: "If God is powerful, then why are we so powerless?" Was the "White man" holding us down? And how do we explain the successes other groups have enjoyed in this free enterprise system that we as a people are still struggling to acquire?

I returned to church but this time as an investigator with a more critical eye. I wanted to re-taste the ingredients within the sermon soup in an effort to determine if there was anything within it that could prove hazardous to our mental health. After visiting churches of various denominations, I discovered a common thread linking the vast majority. Mostly all of them, in my opinion, were preaching a gospel of powerlessness.

Following a long investigative hiatus, I rediscovered this same theological impotence when I relocated to the Atlanta metro area, where I quickly discovered that church was big business. Atlanta has some of the loftiest African American preachers and fanciest churches in the country. After visiting many area churches and continuing on with my investigative tour, I knew the time had come for me to write a book that would shed light on the many psychologically crippling aspects within the church that keeps Blacks in a state of *Holy Lockdown.*

There are basically eight major historically Black Christian churches: African Methodist Episcopal; African Methodist Episcopal Zion; Christian Methodist Episcopal; Church of God in Christ; National Baptist Convention of America; National Baptist Convention, U.S.A.; National Missionary Baptist Convention; and the Progressive National Baptist Convention.

These denominations alone comprise over sixty-five thousand churches and approximately twenty million members. The "Black church," as referenced throughout this book is rooted in the Southern Negro tradition and holds its main services on Sunday mornings (sometimes Saturday), and its members or attendees consider themselves Christians. The Black church is essentially all of the predominately Black Christian congregations. This accounts for the greatest majority of the African American population involved in organized religion. The largest Black denomination, according to the National Baptist Convention U.S.A., is Baptist with well over eight million members.

The church has done many good things and continues to do so. According to an essay previously published entitled "Black Churches and the Inner City Poor" and a shorter version entitled "Supporting Black Church Faith, Outreach and the Inner City Poor," which appeared in the Brookings Review in the Spring of 1999, the church is doing great things. Many Black churches work intensively with at-risk Black youth. In the Washington, D.C. area alone, a six-month field exploration of youth-serving ministries done by Jeremy White and Mary de Marcellus produced evidence that the majority of Black churches had programs such as after school or tutoring programs, evangelization, gang violence prevention, youth groups, and mentoring. But, perhaps, the best known study of African American community involvement was a book published in 1990 by researchers Lincoln and Mamiya titled *The Black Church in the African American Experience*. They reported that of 1,900 ministers and 2,100 churches surveyed, around 71% were engaged in some aspect of community service or outreach program. These included day care centers, job search assistance, substance abuse prevention and food and clothing distribution.

A number of surveys are consistent with the findings of Lincoln and Mamiya. An Atlanta regional survey of Black churches conducted by researcher Naomi Ward and her colleagues cited that out of 150 Black churches in Atlanta, 131 were engaged in extending themselves into the community.

The church, however, is operated by human beings, and no person or institution is above reproach. Although it provides many good things, my objective is to call attention to many of its deficiencies; those things that impede our collective progress. To elaborate on the good of the church would not only have been too consuming but it would have failed to open our eyes to the negative aspects, which are just as important.

Holy Lockdown was written in order to generate awareness in regards to the present dichotomy within our community, which reflects the abundance of Black churches coupled with the abundance of Black problems. As a people, we are far too religious and involved in the church to be experiencing so many social problems. There is something grossly peculiar about this reality. It reflects a detachment of the head from the body; a kind of cultural decapitation within the Black collective. The church is the primary institution among Blacks, but it is obvious, in light of our societal challenges, that the head is not properly communicating with the body.

How can an institution that makes us feel so good and

appears so right, be harmful to us? The church has sometimes been described as being like rat poison—99% sugary, sweet feel-good and only 1% arsenic — but according to a report by Julie Hauserman in the *St. Petersburg Times* "only a pinch of pure arsenic can kill you." The "one percent" that, in a sense, is killing us, is the traditional, non-suspecting things we take for granted.

When we examine the societal ills facing our people, how can one possibly indict the church? I am not suggesting that the church is entirely responsible for all of the negative issues involving Blacks, such as over-consumerism, economic disunity, high rates of hypertension, A.I.D.S., prostate cancer, inner-city violence, or the crisis of the Black prison population. What is suggested here is that the church has a profound impact on many facets of our lives. Most would agree that many problems facing us are a direct result of the injustices of a racist American system at large. Exploitation, discrimination and racial profiling are just some of the staples found in every corner of the United States.

Although societal injustices against Black people are a given, it is nonetheless incumbent upon us to be aware of the vague line in the sand that separates government accountability from self-responsibility. The bottom line is that we may not be so much victims of genocide as we are victims of suicide. Our societal wounds from the self-infliction of incorrect thinking are far greater than those from outer forces (racism) that impede our progress.

The church comes into this picture because since our arrival here in North America and other parts of the world it has had, perhaps, the greatest influence on the collective Black thought process. Our thought process is inherently tied to our behavior. We have dedicated and committed ourselves to the church, more so than any other institution. The vast majority of Black people attend church, and there is no other institution that rivals the church's influence. The church, therefore, is the leader of the people by default. The societal shortcomings of African Americans first begin with a mindset. Whenever people fail to live up to their potential or demonstrate anti-productive behavior, the crime must not only be traced to their actions but to the thoughts of the people prior to their actions. Among other factors, it is primarily the mindset of African Americans that contributes the most to our overall lack of positive production.

Some examples that hinder our lack of production include pumping our dollars outside of our communities, violence toward one another, derogatory language in our music, and engagement in all sorts of regressive behavior. These actions are clear indications of *incorrect thinking*. Although the church is not an advocate of ill behavior, it nonetheless should be held accountable for what it does *not* advocate. If it is not an advocate of intellectual, political, economic or social empowerment, it is guilty of cultural indifference and social apathy.

Liberation must be central to the church's doctrine. Race is relevant because we primarily live, work and worship with other Blacks. Therefore, it seems logical that we should concern ourselves with each other. There is nothing racist about wanting to improve one's race. The colorblind *we are the world* theosophical rhetoric many of our churches promote can only be applied in theory. Our problems are unique, and significant energy must be invested toward solving them.

Since the Black church is one of the biggest influences on the Black collective thought process, it is reasonable to assume that the church would be significantly accountable for our social behavior and would have a major influence upon our cultural attitudes and perspectives. One's behavior is a reflection of one's thoughts. Our mindset requires spotlighting and inventorying. The church, as demonstrated throughout *Holy Lockdown*, provides some of the greatest clues to many of our most fundamental problems.

Over many generations, Blacks have developed an inseparable connection between the sermonic indoctrination that our ears and minds have absorbed and the way we go about handling our daily business. Our ears are one of the doorways into our minds, and information supplied by preachers has been and is still, in many ways, psychologically unfruitful. I do not mean to imply that this has been deliberate, but we as a people are now at the crossroads where we must choose between stagnation and growth. It is time we expand our thinking and usher in the winds of change. Roger Bacon, the English philosopher and scientist, stated, "He that will not apply new remedies must expect new evils."

Note: the term "preacher" throughout this book is used as a generic and general description that includes many of the common names for clergy such as pastor, bishop, minister and reverend.

1

Emotion and Entertainment

The sweet rice is eaten quickly.
– Sierra Leonean Proverb

In Webster's dictionary the word *inspire means to arouse or produce a feeling; to have an animating affect upon.* Fundamentally, aroused feelings and animating affects have been one of the hallmarks in the institution of the Black church. When one is inspired (in a spiritual sense), it can naturally lead to displays of emotion. One of the many reasons we go to church is to get inspired, thereby attaining good feelings and emotional lifts. In a nutshell, the church makes us feel good. It is perceived to be our shelter from the storms of life. We sing, dance, shout, praise, clap, testify, pray, laugh, etc. By the end of the service, after all this activity, many are overcome with emotion.

Sunday service can be both uplifting and emotionally overwhelming. Many people in church become so emotionally affected, they must be physically contained to prevent them from hurting others. Nothing is wrong with becoming emotional or receiving inspiration. Nor is there anything wrong with a safety valve for the desperation that many feel. However, what can and often does happen in an electrically charged atmosphere of high emotion/inspiration is that the exhilarating *feelings and animating effects* generated can easily overshadow or intrude upon the sermonic lesson. This, in turn, affects our reasoning and mental clarity. Our emotionality tends to override progressive learning and critical thinking.

Many people commonly associate the Black church with excessive emotion and theatrical sensationalism. It has also been scrutinized for the lack of practicality within its sermons. Highly emotional behavior, whether at church, in relationships or in confrontations, can cloud one's reasoning. The church, despite the emotion it generates, must maintain its objectivity. That objectivity must also be clearly defined. The church's goals and objectives should always extend into the community, but along with those goals and objectives, churches must demonstrate that the emotionalism is not a goal in itself. It must be part of a sense of reason and practicality, which should be the source of the church's mission. The church has to apply the concept of emotionality going hand-in-hand with practicality. This means that whatever is derived as inspiration in church must be translated and made a part of the pragmatic and thoughtful behavior in one's daily life.

While there is a place for high emotion, at other times emotions within the church should be balanced with rationality. The sermonic message should be captivating, in spite of the theatrics or animation accompanying the message. We have to be able to listen to the sermon with our minds leading the way and not our hearts. When we are made to feel good or become emotional in church, it may inspire us in many positive ways. Feelings, though, are temporary; the way we *think* is more lasting than the way we *feel*.

Karl Marx once said that religion is the opiate of the masses. An opiate, of course, is the relief aid of pain. In a real sense, church has been used as a major pain reliever for Black people.

We must ask ourselves if the high emotions exhibited in church naturally spill over into our actions within society. An overabundance of emotionalism in a system of capitalism does not mix well and has proven to be an exploitable commodity. An Ashanti proverb says, "Wood already touched by fire is not hard to set alight." Commercial manufacturers, well aware of this advantage, prey upon the emotional nature of Black people. With our emotions and hearts leading the way, we have evolved into a race of consumers. We are known to purchase things we really cannot afford and more than likely don't need because material possessions, like the church, makes us *feel* better.

In a society where Black people often feel powerless and subordinate; expensive name brand clothing, pricey cars, and excess material goods serve to compensate for our dearth of power. That, as a consequence, places us collectively in a state of economic dependency.

According to the U.S. Census Bureau, African American consumers have traditionally spent more on name brands, cable subscriptions, food and media. These are things that appeal to the senses and emotions. Blacks make up approximately 12% of the population but only own around 3% of the total wealth of this country. This indicates that much of the "powers" we outwardly project are merely empty *symbols* of power. We must understand that power is where power lies. A good example of symbolic power is when we see young African American males sporting pit bulls at their sides. Among dogs, pit bulls are symbols of strength and power. Another example is the wearing of jewelry with dollar signs. This is an obvious symbol of money, but more accurately, it is symbolic of their aspirations of attaining money.

Black preachers can also be looked upon as symbols of power, since many of them exploit our emotional vulnerabilities. One of a preacher's main objectives is to stir us up, make us shout and have us walking away proclaiming..."That man can preach!" If he lectured us calmly there would not be much of an audience the following Sunday. This should cause us to wonder just how much of his sermon is truly for the people, and how much is for his own advancement.

I once asked a White co-worker to attend church with me. He quickly responded by saying, "Oh, no! I can't go to one of those *fall-out* churches." While not all Black churches display the emotional fervor to which he referred, the potential is always there, especially in an emotionally charged atmosphere. This does not suggest that churches should operate in a quiet manner like libraries. Expressive displays of emotion are good and can be therapeutic, but it has to lead to a practical place over time. It has to lead to a usefulness of some sort. We have to have religion with reason and emotion with a purpose.

Take a glass of water for example. If we place two or three tablespoons of salt in a glass, stir it up vigorously and wait for a few minutes, some of the salt will dissolve but much of it will settle to the bottom of the glass. This is symbolically what happens to the Black collective (the salt of the earth) who are frequently stirred up in the church, which represents the cleansing affects of water. We are routinely stirred up in the church, yet we are consistently settling to the bottom of society.

African Americans have one of the highest school dropout rates and more males in prison than college. We also wield the highest percentage of H.I.V. cases, unemployment, and homicide. Blacks, in general, are notorious churchgoers and have been attending churches in droves for centuries. Why do we have so many churches and so many problems? Where is this theatrical, emotional theology leading us? It is okay to feel good and receive spiritual uplifting. It is also pointless, however, for Blacks to keep winning individual salvation battles yet keep losing societal wars.

One of the latest religious studies conducted by Barna, a religious researching organization, indicates that more than half of all African Americans attend church regularly. The study also indicated that the typical Black church has an average attendance that is about 50% greater than that of the typical White church. Other studies indicate some 82% of Blacks (versus 67% of Whites) are church members, 82% of Blacks (versus 55% of Whites) say that religion is very important in their lives and 86% of Blacks (versus 60% of Whites) believe that religion "can answer all or most of today's problems."

Most of us, to some degree, have been influenced by the Black church and are a current mental product of its indoctrination. It is time we explore the connection between what we are receiving inside the church and what we are transmitting outside the church. Our sacred input must be reflected in our secular output. Stirring people up and sensationalizing them week after week, year after year and generation after generation does not necessarily translate into progressive and productive behavior. Continuously being emotionally roused by a "good" preacher only guarantees that we will continue to be entertained.

Despite the reality of racism and the systematic hurdles America has placed before us, much of our overall condition can be attributed to our incorrect and misguided thinking. We are products of our thoughts. We have to *think* that it is our responsibility to manufacture our own products, educate our children, resist drugs and stop killing one another. Accomplishing these things requires correct thinking. We (the salt of the earth) cannot continue to crawl inside of a glass of water (church), get stirred up and return to our same conditions at the bottom of the glass in this free enterprise system. We cannot keep expecting miracles from God to change our circumstances. We empower ourselves by thinking logically, not by becoming emotional. A book written by Robert Greene and Joost Elfers entitled *The 48 Laws of Power,* explains how emotion can be counterproductive when striving for power. The book states:

> An emotional response to a situation is the single greatest barrier to power, a mistake that will cost you a lot more than any temporary satisfaction you might gain by expressing your feelings. Emotions cloud reason, and if you cannot see the situation clearly, you cannot prepare for and respond to it with any degree of control.

I once heard a preacher say that those in church who do not worship with high intensity, have not been through any hard times. He stated that the calm, objective, non-emotional church attendee has not had any great obstacle in life that he or she has overcome. That remark is an unfair assumption. How does he know what one has been through in their lives, or have overcame? Life challenges all of us. Just because one shouts and worships with highly emotional intensity does not mean they have experienced more tribulations than those who do not.

Many of us are familiar with the classic gospel song by Shirley Ceasar entitled *"Hold My Mule."* It is the story about an old man named John who joined a dignified church. The members considered him too crude because he was excessively emotional, and shouted and testified too much. A few of the well-to-do members decided to go to John's house to tell him they no longer wanted him in their church. They were tired of his undignified approach to worshiping. One day the old man was plowing in the field and saw the men drive up onto his land. He knew exactly why they had come. John made the men aware of the many blessings that God had bestowed upon him and told one of the men to hold his mule because if they would not permit him to shout in their church, he would shout right then and there.

Caesar's song is one of the most beloved and popular

songs in Black gospel music. It has served as a kind of support system for all of the "shouting Johns" in our churches. Many congregants often feel cheated if the preacher is unable to generate the excitability to which they have grown accustomed. We are cheated, however, when we cannot harness our emotional energy attained at church and transfer that emotion into something sensible and practical.

It is impossible to discuss the emotional nature of the church without exploring the role entertainment plays within it. The reactions generated by preachers are similar to those generated by hip-hop, R&B, and rock stars. The crying, hysteria, shouting, passing out and dancing are similar to what happens at many popular concerts. The preacher *must* incorporate entertainment within his sermon. It is a tried and tested method, proven to yield great returns on his investments. The church can be a very entertaining institution, and many preachers have developed a flare for the dramatic.

Many preachers calculatingly put on sensational "dog and pony" shows for their congregations. These "shows" are of prime-time quality and, because of their mass appeal, can be considered some of the "greatest shows on earth." Preachers have been known to crawl on the floor, carry large crosses on their backs, parade back and forth, jump up and down, sing, dance, act and even stage miracles.

Dr. Amos Jones, author of the book *As You Go Preach*, provides many examples on how to deliver more exciting and dramatic sermons. Preaching, sermon building, tithe solicitation, membership recruiting, maintaining and captivating a congregation are all taught in various theological schools. Books that teach preaching techniques with suggestions on sermon building, delivery, and stirring congregations can be found on the market. A Black preacher without theatrics is in danger of becoming a preacher without a congregation. It has come to be expected by them.

There are names for many of these styles and techniques used by our leaders of the church. For instance, "whooping" is a technique where the preacher, usually near the conclusion of his sermon, incorporates (often with the organist) a slurred tone in his delivery that sings the ending words of his phrases. Whooping is a sentence that crescendos sometimes into an *"uuuhhh, aaahhh"* kind of climax. The late Reverend C.L. Franklin used it very effectively and influenced its popularity. It has been one of the greatest sensationalizing and effective tools used by Black preachers and regarded as an irreplaceable spoon for stirring up and keeping congregations on the edge of their seats.

Preaching styles are normally learned through observation. When it comes to preaching, the novice learns his or her craft by making continuous trips to monkey-see-monkey-do ville. Over time, Black preachers have picked up various crafts and techniques from watching the most colorful and dynamic among their peers.

Frederick "Reverend Ike" Eikerenkoetter who is often called the father of television evangelism and is famous for wearing expensive suits, driving fancy cars and generating lots of money, has helped to influence the fine art of pastoral ostentation. Many phrases and expressions are routinely copied. Such phrases as "look at the person next to you and say...," "y'all didn't hear me" and saying "amen" after every sentence are very popular and have been copied by many preachers. The expression "watch this" has also become catchy. Whenever preachers tell congregations to look to the person next to them and say whatever they request, the preacher obtains immediate power from this gesture. His power is fueled by having hundreds or thousands of people instantly do what's commanded. Also, such a gesture can serve as a needed power move for what may not be such a powerful sermon.

I once witnessed a preacher shout, "You mad at yo' spouse. You mad at yo' co-workers. You mad at yo' children." That particular technique is referred to as a "run." Runs are probably the most common method used by preachers. It repeats the first few words of each sentence and changes the ending. By using runs, preachers effectively build up more and more tension on the way to the finale. Musicians use this technique to accomplish the same dramatic affect in building up tension right before the climax. After his run of "You mad at yo'...," he climaxed it by shouting, "Instead of you bein' mad at the world, you need to be mad at the devil for givin' you the mindset to be mad at somebody!" He then paraded into a semi-dance that consequently "brought down the house." Nothing he said was so eloquent and profound as to produce the type of congregational outburst he received. It was how he dramatized his words that caused the congregation to respond in such a manner. Outbursts over insignificant or average sermonic remarks are very common. We have to realize that much of a preacher's popularity is based on their ability to entertain. It is not always in the substance of *what* they say, but *how* they say it.

Black preachers are known for shouting at adults to get their points across. This is an act of condescension. Black congregants whose preachers shout at them are unconsciously demoted to the role of children. Like children, they attend church only to be chastised and ridiculed by their shouting preachers through a process of sermonic implication. Many preachers cleverly point out a "sin" of which they know anyone in general may be "guilty" of committing. After the implication, preachers may say something like—"Ya'll got awfully quiet all of a sudden" or "I must have struck a nerve in somebody" or "I see some folks squirmin' in their seats."

Indirect ridicule through implication is a very effective technique/trick that preachers use to give the impression that their sermons are effectively hitting home or are in tune with our personal lives. We are calculatingly being led in the direction most advantageous for the preacher.

We cannot attend church as empty jugs waiting to be filled. The emptier our jugs the more susceptible we are to being sermonically exploited. We are adults who benefit from being taught and not tricked. Pastors have a good understanding of human psychology. They know what emotional buttons to push and when to push them. They must be able to anticipate how people will react to their sermons. We do not have to attend church with a cynical attitude, but we must be aware of what is actually being said and done. Remember, we are in church and not at the circus or a magic show. Do not apologize for being totally objective when listening to preachers. Sermons must possess more substance and less sensationalism. There is enough entertainment within the music to keep us emotionally aroused.

For example, notice whenever the lead singer from the choir performs a solo; no matter what words the soloist actually sings, the congregation is much more likely to react emotionally based on how the soloist *sounds*. The words the soloist sings may indeed have merit; but, it is not the words the soloist sings that causes reactions, but the beauty in the *sound* emerging from his or her voice. They could sing "aaahhh" or "oooohh" and if it *sounds* good, they will get a lively reaction from the congregation. Emotional reactions are thereby generated based on the quality of *sound* and *feel* of the music, not necessarily the words. This is another example of entertainment being such an integral part of the church. Many people go to church to hear the beautiful music. They find it satisfying, fulfilling and as equally enjoyable as the actual sermon.

At the conclusion of Sunday service, the pastor usually beckons to unsaved souls or non-members to get saved or join the church. This is where the music takes on a spiritually seductive and sensationalizing initiative. Pastors make gallant attempts to seduce non-members to join and/or get saved. He accomplishes this with his right hand man—the organist. At this moment, there is a fine line between recruiting souls and subtly creating an atmosphere of guilt. The preacher is the fisherman, and the organist is the bait. Together they reel you in with *hook, line and sinker*. Similar to a dramatic scene in a movie, if the music were taken out, the scene would not be nearly as powerful.

Music during and at the conclusion of a sermon is a vital ingredient and generates more intensity and spiritual ecstasy than the preacher could ever do alone. Music is the honey during and after the sermon that catches the bees. When the preacher gets on a roll and begins to pick up sermonic steam, the organist often backs or supports this intensity by incorporating various gospel licks or short musical phrases that, in a sense, applauds or co-signs the preacher's message.

As far as music being a part of a worshipping atmosphere, the Black Muslims of the Nation of Islam understand the potential distraction of music and prohibit its use in many Mosques. There is a proper place and time for music and entertainment and sometimes we misuse its purpose. For instance, every year in Atlanta, an annual business event is open to the public. The primary purpose of this affair is to introduce businesses, network and sell products or services. The focus of this event, and similar Black business events, often gets shifted to the entertainment segment of the function. These events may have business intentions, but they eventually merge into parties. Music groups are invited to perform and often wind up stealing the show because more energy is directed toward the music rather than the main objective of the event.

Preachers understand that regardless of whether our gatherings are sacred or secular, Blacks seem to have an insatiable desire to be entertained. If preachers ignore this critical characteristic, they may have difficulty inspiring congregants to become members of their churches. Many of them feel a sense of disappointment if their sermon, coupled with their acts of entertainment, fails to ignite the emotional flames of the congregation.

It is disappointing that a preacher's ability to excite and arouse is often worth more than their ability to educate and lead. Many erroneously attribute the emotional atmosphere in church to the presence of God, believing that the high emotion displayed in church is a sign of the Holy Spirit. Isn't it ironic that the "presence of God" becomes more profound the more preachers incorporate entertainment, theatrics and sensationalizing tactics into their sermons? How often would the "Holy Spirit" show its presence in the church if pastors preached the exact same sermon but delivered it void of the repetition, animation, shouting and showmanship?

Church is an entertaining experience, but there are long-term consequences to pay for spiritual shenanigans. Church takes on a different meaning when emotion and entertainment cloud objectivity or is camouflaged under the pretext of something else.

2 Rhetorical Confinement

Fine words do not produce food.
– Nigerian Proverb

Rhetorical confinement is a term used to describe the non-progressive and stagnant language within Black sermons. Sermonic rhetoric has been trapped on a stationary spinning wheel for many generations. Black preachers, in terms of sermonic language, are in the recycling business. The absence of vernacular evolution within the church has helped to stifle the development and growth of Black people.

In my lifetime, I have visited many churches and watched many services on television. Sometimes, in addition to highlighting my Bible, I took notes regarding teachings I heard in church and things I felt could be pragmatically applied to improve my life. I must admit I have learned a great deal in church. Nevertheless, what I have found most striking over the years is how redundant the sermons can be. The church has been one of the biggest influences on our culture and thought process, yet it remains rudimentary in its arsenal of useful ideas.

How often have we attended church and heard *basically* the same re-heated language over and over again? Some of the sermons are delivered more or less eloquently or may come from a more persuasive or bombastic preacher. Other sermons may be framed, formatted, dramatized or phrased a little differently; but far too often, we are hearing sermonic re-runs.

For generations, Black preachers have been shouting and sweating out the same trite rhetoric from their pulpits. It is amazing to hear similar expressions from so many different preachers over the years. The sermonic rhetoric of the new breed of national and international preachers may sound somewhat more intriguing on the surface, but when the new clothes (language) are stripped away, we are left with a body familiar to us.

The church rhetoric can sound like a broken record. It is apparent that preachers quite naturally run out of things to preach about and are severely limited in terms of introducing us to more progressive and stimulating doctrines. They are often forced to manufacture the intensity within the sermon. They must, in a sense, make something interesting of something quite ordinary. Preachers have to be skilled in improvising.

Because of an insufficient supply of ready to order sermons, preachers cleverly employ "fillers" in the body of their sermons. These are bread and butter scriptures, phrases or popular clichés that preachers throw in their sermon soup, which are known for getting emotional and affirmative reactions from congregations. Fillers are effective in eating up the clock and directing preachers out of rhetorical traffic jams. They are comparable to certain foods that may give you a full and satisfying feeling but are lacking in nutrition. We may leave church with feelings of being full but, to a large degree, we have only been stuffed with non-nutritional, reheated leftovers.

Repetition is the anchor of the Black preacher's sermonic repertoire. Their survival depends on it. Repetition, however, is often camouflaged and condiments are added to the sermon to spice it up, in the hope that it won't be recognized as last week's leftovers. The church, as with any other business, understands that familiarity breeds confidence. Preachers stick to rhetoric they know will produce "Amens." When they are uninspired or unprepared to deliver original five star sermons, they can always reach into the deep well of Negro tradition and pull out an "old reliable." Sermons such as these serve as oratorical anchors and are valuable for keeping preachers from drifting too far out into deeper unfamiliar waters. These types of sermons lend themselves to improvisation and are full of allegories that create vivid imagery. The books of the New Testament are often the preacher's main choice because they graphically illustrate the life of Jesus and are less esoteric than the stories in the Old Testament.

It is challenging for preachers to be creative in a genre so steeped in tradition. During slavery, sermons were preached with the intent of making us *feel* better about our lowly positions. Unfortunately, many Blacks accepted their plight and were powerless in a White authoritative and cruel system. In the eyes of many preachers, they saw no point in preaching a gospel that would encourage Black liberation, progress or unity. Slaves were divided and scattered amongst southern plantations and discouraged from starting family units. Many preachers were faced with the necessity of centering on the *one day Jesus will deliver us* type of messages.

Today, Black preachers are still delivering sermons designed to make us feel better. They continue to deliver sermons that do not have a lot to do with Black progress and liberation. The church rituals and sermonic vernacular are locked inside of a time capsule, unable to recognize that the world and Black people have significantly changed. Preachers are still trying to get the same old dogs (sermonic rhetoric) to hunt. Old dogs, however, quit hunting after a while.

Sermons have gotten a little more creative over the years, thanks in part to the computer age. A variety of biblical software is available to assist preachers. They can input any word or phrase and unearth its exact location within the Bible. Preachers are also becoming more biblically informative with the advent of Bible dictionaries and concordances. Essentially, with the right tools and adequate improvisational skills, many of us can effectively elaborate on stories within the Bible.

Preachers must be ever mindful of the progress being made within their daily or weekly sermonic messages. Future generations should not have to listen to recycled rhetoric more suited to stirring up people than it is for building up people. We need to examine our own experiences. The next time we attend church, when the service has ended, let us think about whether we truly learned something new. Reflect on the message and whether it possessed something that could lead to tangible changes in our lives. Ponder its usefulness and relevance. Determine whether the preacher just found a new way of saying an old thing.

Most of us with significant life tenure have acquired a vast amount of life experience. Life tenure teaches us valuable lessons and reveals many things to us. It is our choice whether or not we take heed of life's lessons. There are certainly more life lessons we will experience, but most of us have learned a great deal from the school of hard knocks. Preachers are no different than the rest of us and have learned in much the same manner. We are experienced adults, and if we are truly honest with ourselves, we will see that most of the things flowing out of our preacher's mouths are teachings with which we are already familiar.

At times we are truly enlightened to something different and substantial, but far too often following an informative statement, preachers begin to beat us over our heads with situational examples that serve to validate their point. It is akin to teaching a child that fire burns. There is no end, however, to the countless examples exemplifying the fact that fire can burn. To continue to drive home a point until the people reach a satisfactory level on the emotional meter seems condescending. Sermons of this nature abound in the Black church. They are the kind whereby the preacher reads a few scriptures out of the Bible, closes it, and then proceeds to take off on the path of *situational substantiation*.

Good points are insufficient if there is no growth behind them. You can place a dot (point) on a piece of paper and draw an infinite number of lines crossing through it; the point, though, does not move.

Many preachers choose a particular theme or subject and begin to expound upon it. For instance, the day's message or topic of the sermon may be *Preparing for the Harvest* or *Being Like an Oak Tree in the Presence of the Devil.* Often preachers refer to their Bibles, concordances and software, then input the words that are contained within the particular title. The concordance or software locates in the Bible the particular words in the title of the day's topic. He then reads the related scriptures and attempts to parlay the sermon into an interesting and meaningful message. A preacher milks the time in order to stretch the sermon out to whenever it is scheduled to end. They are able to do this because of their shrewd gift of gab, creative improvisational skills and because they expound upon topics based on everyday situations to which all of us can relate. Edward P. Wimberly explains in his book *African American Pastoral Care*, how Black pastors are able to effectively relate to their congregations.

> [Wimberly writes]Black pastors use many types of stories—long stories, anecdotes, short sayings, metaphors—to respond to the needs of their parishioners. Most specific instances in life situations lend themselves to story formation. For example, stories can be used to address the normal crises people face daily, such as birth, a child's first day at school or at day care; transitions from childhood to adolescence to adulthood; mid-life, old age, and death transitions.

Many lessons can be learned from everyday situations and incorporated into the day's topic. This kind of preaching seems superficial and an over-simplified method of ministering. Some preachers lack the substance of true leadership and this causes speculation as to whether they were actually "called" to preach. True leaders have vision and are able to impart information to us capable of bringing about progressive change. Blacks, it seems, in areas such as family structure, elderly respect, musical knowledge, etc., are regressing. One of the primary reasons for this (in addition to the deficiencies within the home) is due to lack of true leadership.

Something must be distinctly different about a preacher/leader before they are placed in positions of power. They must have an uncanny, fresh and unique way of looking at life that is easily recognized by the people. Martin Luther King Jr. had that quality and so did Elijah Muhammad, Marcus Garvey and Haile Selassie. Preachers do not necessarily have to be on the grand scale or shoulder the responsibilities as did these great men, but they are nonetheless leaders.

Many preachers have evolved into pulpit capitalists. They capitalize on the idea that we *perceive* them to be men of God. One of the greatest tools preachers possess in establishing power is having the people perceive them as powerful. They capitalize on our emotional vulnerabilities. Habitual, emotional reactions from congregations help to foster this perception and only contribute to their showmanship. They are content in knowing that we have had our emotional cup filled. Every Sunday is like an encore performance.

Preachers also capitalize on our financial vulnerabilities.

They often use the "if you give you will get" and "get ready for the harvest" trick to acquire our dollars. They tell us that when we give we will receive. This teaching is a backward concept. Giving does not translate into receiving. We receive so that we may give. By examining universal principles we find that the earth must first *receive* the information from the sun and rain in order to *give* us fruit and vegetation. If a person shares his or her knowledge, they have to first *receive* it before they can share it. Ask—not *give* and we will receive. How many of us have given money to someone but have yet to receive any of it back? When we give something to someone we must have it in order to give. Simply put, you cannot give something you don't have.

Preachers keep their congregations locked in a mode of giving. We must learn to be receptors. When we are in a receptive mode we are conduits for information—which is where power truly lies. Countless people do not attend church or donate money to it, yet they are abundantly blessed. Giving does not only pertain to money. We can give our time, effort, advice and our friendship. The money we tithe in church does not magically guarantee our lives will be better. Many people faithfully tithe ten percent or more of their income, but are consistently broke.

Preachers also capitalize on our ignorance. Many of us, with practice and the right kind of biblical tools, can perform acts similar to what preachers do every Sunday. But we are led to believe that the information our preachers provide to us is at the peak of profundity. True profundity, leaves profound impacts. Where is all of our "profundity" leading us? Leadership is the art of identifying a problem and working hard toward solving it. It is not preaching; it is teaching and *showing* the way. Leadership is having a vision beyond what most people envision and showing them how to get there.

Remember that preachers are part entertainer and similar, in many ways, to recording artists. Artists are under specific contracts, which require them to produce a certain amount of recordings during the contract period. To avoid breaches, artists are often forced to shell out pieces of sub par work. Preachers, in an implied sense, are contractually obligated to pull rabbits out of hats every Sunday morning and on other days of the week. They face the same obligation dilemmas as recording artists and produce stacks of filler sermons that are merely desperate attempts to keep their congregations entertained.

One over-used filler and irresponsible remark by Black preachers many of us have heard is "I don't care how smart you are, how much you think you know or how many degrees you have, if you don't have Jesus, you don't have nothing." That remark is dangerous because it lets us off the intellectual hook. One may interpret it as meaning we do not necessarily *need* science, math, geography, physics and art as long as we've got Jesus. This kind of preaching can have harmful implications. Why would a preacher utter such language to a people once prohibited by law from learning to read? Our youth are already behind many other groups in several scholastic areas and are not competing at the academic levels at which they are capable. This is not because of intellectual inferiority. The youth are tied to a legacy of damaging sermonic indoctrination that thwarts their natural intellectual capabilities.

I once heard an Atlanta based preacher state that if you were to lock two men in separate rooms and provide one of the men with a Bible and the other with a thousand books, the man with the Bible would turn out to be more powerful than the man that read the thousand books. The preacher's rationale for this was that the man who read the thousand books would only have knowledge whereas the man who read the Bible would have wisdom. How can the preacher be so sure of this? Much more important though, is why the preacher is entertaining such a scenario like that in the first place. It is not necessarily what you read that matters but how you *apply* what you read. This demonstrates our willingness to sidestep cerebrally challenging paths toward intellect. Too many of us have chosen to crawl along the path that leads to mental laziness and emotional comfort.

What is even more ironic about the abundance of sermons that irresponsibly promote Bible-over-book-smart messages, is that the early Black churches merged the two concepts together. They viewed education as the primary key to our success in America and often doubled as schools. Black children often learned to read and write in Sunday school. Morehouse College began as a school in the basement of the Springfield Baptist Church in Augusta, Georgia, and Spelman was founded in the basement of Friendship Baptist Church in Atlanta. The great Tuskegee University started as a small room across from the AME Zion Church in Tuskegee, Alabama. Black colleges like Fisk and Howard also had religious (church) roots.

Preachers, nowadays, have become rudimentary rousers, and most do not seem to recognize they are in positions that require insight and intellect. They must be thorough men and women of the cloth. They must be able to serve the people by providing and promoting spiritual, intellectual, economic and social growth. To accomplish this great task, preachers would benefit from having a general and well-rounded knowledge of many important and relevant subjects such as Black and world history, geography, social studies, business, politics, current events, philosophy, science and art.

Far too many of us today read the Bible to the exclusion of everything else. This limits our literary exposure and diversity. Reading only the Bible makes us information poor. We consider the Bible the final authority and the definitive manual for living because this is the idea we have been presented with all of our lives. We have rode the horse that was in our stable.

If someone gave you a shoe heel instead of a hammer to drive a nail in a wall, you would use what you were provided. As far as the religious or spiritual information we receive in church, many of us only know what we have been told and have only bought what we have been sold. This statement applies to many of our pastors that have not researched other fascinating systems of thought that lay beyond the parameters of what they were raised to believe.

We must keep in mind that our belief systems or perceived truth, is "truth" from *our* frame of reference and are based on our conditioned views of truth. Our ways of interpreting and applying the sermonic rhetoric of our pastors are correct from the perspective where we are sitting.

Although there are exceptions to everything, four factors normally determine a person's religious or spiritual beliefs. The first is geography. For example, people born and raised in Spain, are most likely to be Roman Catholic. Those who live in Japan have an excellent chance of either being adherents of Shintoism or Buddhism. Historical circumstances are another factor. Had Africans not been kidnapped and transported to North America, Blacks might not have been exposed to Christianity in such a way. Had Arabs not invaded parts of Africa, it may not have its current Muslim population.

The third factor is tradition. If our parents were Catholic, Muslim, Jew, etc., then it is very probable we will adopt those same beliefs. A final factor is accessibility. Here in the United States, it is much easier to find affiliations with popular religious organizations and beliefs systems such as Baptist, Muslim, Catholic, etc., than it is to find affiliations with traditional African or more unconventional spiritual organizations.

These facts are necessary to mention, not for the purpose of attacking or prying us from our current beliefs, but to open our minds to the reality that what we believe is not so much of our own design but from many influences we may not have considered. Our "truth" then, is purely relative.

Hold on if we must to our current religious or spiritual beliefs and concepts, but embellish and expound upon them. We have to enhance our thinking, broaden our perspectives and also allow ourselves to be open to other formidable ideas, concepts and possibilities of thought. What our pastors preach should be larger in scope. Although we live locally, we must think globally and see ourselves in connection with the rest of the world.

Ineffective preaching translates into ineffective people

because the main source of many faithful churchgoers' exposure to inspirational or educational figures basically comes from their local pastors. Their primary source and pursuits toward higher learning (other than job or school related) are relegated to the literature of the Bible.

A lack of exposure to other great literature and infinite worlds of thought results in many churchgoers perceiving their pastor's sermons as prophetic. To the enlightened, however, they are very ordinary and basic. This affects us tremendously because another recent survey conducted by Barna, indicated that 63% of Blacks believe their pastors are the most important leaders in the community.

A preacher once gave a sermon about the rise and fall of various nations in the Bible and how these particular nations fell from glory. He stated that the primary cause of decline for most of these nations was because they failed to give God the glory for their powerful positions. He used the United States as an example of a nation that has been abundantly blessed but is now in danger of losing her power because she has forgotten the many blessings God has bestowed upon her. He alluded to the victories in war "God" had enabled the United States to win. He used the Great Depression of the 1920s and '30s as an example of how God loosed the United States from the jaws of despondency and resuscitated America into a strong and mighty nation. The preacher boasted about

America being the land of plenty and proclaimed it as the greatest and most powerful nation on earth. God, he said, would once again rescue America from the September 11th crisis. The point of his message was that even though we are blessed with riches, we must always acknowledge God as the reason for the blessings.

On the surface, there was nothing wrong with the basic intent of his message, but it seemed apparent that the preacher lacked a global perspective and historical understanding as to how these various nations, particularly the United States, came to power. Yes, America is a great nation, but there are various reasons behind her greatness. Everything that appears to be good about this nation did not necessarily come as a result of God's divine blessings. America's powerful position has been shaped by hundreds of years of an *ungodly* governmental institution that benefited from free Black labor. Slavery provided the basis and foundation for wealth in America. We must also account for the murderous acts of aggression toward Native Americans from whom this "blessed" land was stolen. And least we forget, a little thing called foreign policy, an area where the United States has been less than godly on many occasions.

Perhaps the preacher knew about these historical atrocities; perhaps he didn't. But purposely withholding or intentionally sidestepping pertinent facts for the sake of his sermon, in an attempt to create a picture that would validate his sermonic point, is not demonstrating leadership. This is a form of sermonic capitalism and exploitation.

Preachers need to know the deeper meanings of spiritual matters, so they can impart the right information to their congregations. Preachers misconstrue meanings or take many Biblical passages out of context. This is exemplified in Proverbs 3:5 which reads "lean not unto thine own understanding." A meaningful passage, but like many other biblical passages, it has evolved into a church cliché. This verse has been quoted frequently in the Black church, and because it is taken too literally, it is often irrationally applied. Upon exploring the deeper meaning of this passage, does "lean not unto thine own understanding" mean we are not supposed to think for ourselves, invent, or approach life with an insatiable curiosity?

When subjects like philosophy, mythology, science, metaphysics, astrology, or astronomy are mentioned to many Black Christians, they proclaim that these studies are "of man," "worldly," or "carnal." This attitude toward knowledge and abstract thought is a perpetuation of the big lie handed down to Blacks during slavery when we were prevented from learning to read. The slave master's consensus was that we would be happier and more content if we knew less and lived simpler lives serving White people. Because of this lie and the fact that many slaves did not aspire to read or write (because of the danger it imposed), it was very easy for them to develop a distaste for higher learning. Philosophy, astronomy, astrology, etc., were brushed off as being the stuff of the devil, and many churches are still perpetuating this lie. Our ignorance of these important and relevant subjects gives rise to our apathy toward them. What we do not know can hurt us. Having knowledge about these subjects in no way detracts from our spirituality. In many ways, they enhance it.

It is ironic that the everyday lives we lead are essentially dependent upon creative thinking, "independent" pursuits of knowledge, and our "own" understanding of the natural world. In previous generations, Blacks commonly regarded topics such as space exploration, genetic study, or biological research as "tampering with God's work." Some churches have and continue to openly object to the advancement of science and technology. Psychologically speaking, Black preachers may have naively helped to place thorn bushes in the career paths of many Black youth who, potentially, may have had interests in the technical and scientific fields.

Consider something as simple as our cell phones. They exist and operate as a result of human intelligence having the know-how to place satellites several miles into space. The utilization of microwaves, radio waves and x-rays enable us to cook and heat our food, listen to the radio, watch television and see the insides of our anatomy. Cars, planes, spacecrafts, computers and robots exist because of our technological understanding.

The church has very subtly denounced brainpower, but we take full advantage of the multitude of conveniences it brings into our lives. We are riding on the backs of great thinkers, those people that did not receive all of their knowledge or inspiration from the Bible. Many Christians try to explain that "lean not unto thine own understanding" means that we are not supposed to walk the path or live our lives according to the way *we* think is right but walk the path that God has laid out for us. Some Biblical verses cannot be tossed around so loosely, and preachers must not assume that congregations will interpret them correctly. Passages like "lean not unto thine own understanding" have to be thoroughly explained and correctly interpreted, to assure its meaning is not misconstrued.

We cannot just praise our way into productivity. We cannot worship our way into competing in this technologically advanced world. Eventually Black people are going to have to question the relevance of what our pastors are preaching. Can we take the information home and eat it, pay our rent with it, or make a financial profit with it? On the other hand, does the preaching just make us feel better, give us hope, comfort us and tell us that everything is going to be okay?

Also, if getting to heaven is our main goal, then we will only be creating a hell for ourselves here on earth. We live on earth and improving our conditions here has to be our main priority. Our sacred goals must make secular sense.

Preachers are in very trusting positions and have the power to elevate or reduce the human spirit. They have to take on responsibilities far greater than just arousing our emotions.Through means of sermonic rhetorical confinement, the church has helped to quell the imaginations of Blacks. Rudimentary sermons have entangled many of us in a web of simple-mindedness. We are habitually mesmerized by the same basic sermonic language heard many times before. It is a language many of us already intuitively know.

It is common to hear preachers condescendingly make use of sermonic fillers by warning us about how "when we get right with God we're going to lose our friends, and people are going to start talking about us." Other common sermons are about "people who start to think they are better than us because they've got more money or material possessions." More frequent filler sermons are concerned with "who our true friends are," how "different we'll walk and talk once we start living for the Lord," "the bad attitudes we bring to work and have toward each other," and how we "continue to hold grudges with one another." There are the trite and traditional expressions such as "He's a doctor in the sick room and a lawyer in the courtroom";"He may not come when you want Him to, but He's always right on time"; "God won't put no more on us than we can bear";"If God is for you, who can be against you"; "He's better to me than I've been to myself"; "Weeping may endure for a night, but joy cometh in the morning"; and "Greater is He that is in me, than he that is in the world." We also sing the same hymns repeatedly.

Faithful churchgoers have stated that although we may indeed inherently or intuitively know and have heard much of what is preached, it is important for it to be reiterated and reinforced, mainly for inspirational purposes. The real question is why are we in such constant need of reinforcement? What is this mental hole within us that requires regular filling? Why do we need to be consistently reminded to do right?

Yes, we do need to consistently feed our spirits, but we are nonetheless adults, and unlike children, should not have to be continuously prodded to be good and do "right." Our real concerns should be what we are *doing* outside the church, not what we are *hearing* in it. Fifty years from now, will we go to church, hear dynamic, emotionally uplifting sermons, yet find ourselves in an even worse societal position than we are today?

Our current predicament reveals our childlike nature. The fact that we are too dependent upon other groups to provide for us validates this. We are a financially irresponsible race of consumers. The condescending, redundant and counterrevolutionary sermonic language within the church helps to perpetuate our childlike nature. Blacks desire what they perceive they lack, and if we crave redundant preaching, then maybe it is because a perception has evolved that we are lacking in much.

Consider our childlike language in the very things we desire God to do, such as "lead me on," "watch over me," "guide me," "walk with me," "deliver (child birth) me," "save me," "you promised me that you would never leave me," "you said you would," "mold me," "comfort me," "do with me as you will," and "hold my hand." Such requests, regardless of whom they are directed toward, are bound to have a subliminal effect on the subconscious.

Language is very powerful, and we are strongly affected by the words we speak and the thoughts we possess. Psychologists have long been interested in the relationship between language and thought. Benjamin Whorf, in the book simply titled, *Psychology an Introduction* by Benjamin B. Lahey, proposes that the structure of one's language influences the way he or she thinks. Whorf states that "even if language and thought were not synonymous, the fact that much thinking is in the form of language, raises the possibility that the structure of language could influence thinking in some way."

We become what we speak, and we remain as children when we continue to speak as children. A common argument to this is that God is our Father, and we are His children and should communicate with our Father as a child would to its father. How have these helpless pleas with pitiful victim overtones benefited us when it comes to Black productivity? Much of the language our preachers encourage us to speak and thoughts they encourage us to possess, only perpetuates our needy "Lord, help me" outlook on life. We have to know that we possess godlike abilities and are capable of achieving anything. This should be easy to accept since we have been taught that, "In God all things are possible" (Mark:10:27).

Our language and childlike requests denote powerlessness. It is the kryptonite that immobilizes our super beings within. Blacks have been theologically raised on the idea they are powerless and that real power lies in the realm of the supernatural. Because there is a major absence of metaphoric understanding within the church, we have believed that only biblical prophets can part seas, slay giants and walk on water. Childishly, and ironically speaking, we must first know that we obtain power by summoning forth the keys to our "Little Red Engines" that *think* we can.

The language of the sermons within the church has not, over generations, adequately expounded on the godlike powers within us. Preachers have siphoned into our psyches that we are utterly helpless in and of ourselves and we are made whole only in Jesus. This denial of self has deeply affected our perceptions of one another as well. We lack collective confidence in terms of what we think we are capable of accomplishing as a unit. We are programmed to wait for the miracle to effect change. We have been made to believe our fate and even our negative behavior is somehow God's will. If everything is God's will then that means God is going to do what He wants to anyway; why ask Him for anything? Our language is the vehicle that drives our action, or in the case of Black people, our inaction.

We have been sermonized into children in the literal sense. Children do not take responsibility for their own actions or problems. They "lay their burdens down" as we have been taught to do by our preachers. This is passive, counterrevolutionary preaching. Our burdens are our own, and we must deal with them ourselves. Overcoming and facing our own burdens, builds cultural character and forces us to be responsible for our own actions.

It is not an accident our songs are saturated with the word "baby," and our young adults wear their pants down to their knees (like children). Also, like children, we have limited knowledge of money, and, as a consequence, we irresponsibly consume beyond our means. Like children, Blacks consume the most junk food. Our men refer to their friends as home-*boys*, their houses as cribs and we litter where we live. Despite the fact that many other "minority" groups have flourished, Blacks are still collectively stuck on the bottom rungs of the societal totem pole. We have been "babyfied" into comfortable sermonic cradles and wrapped snuggly in "it's going to be all right, Jesus will take care of me" sermonic blankets.

Far too many of our neighborhoods are inundated with unsightly debris. Trashing where we live is not only indicative of an impoverished mentality but is also one of the most irresponsible and childish displays of behavior we exhibit. Littering speaks volumes. When Blacks throw empty soda cans, beer bottles, or potato chip bags on the ground in their (or any other) neighborhood, it symbolizes many of our shortcomings. Besides the obvious clues of non-ownership and lack of pride, it also implies a lack of environmental consciousness. It indicates that we are oblivious to how our cluttered environment creates negative perceptions about us. We shoot ourselves in the foot when we litter because filth attracts filth. Our mentalities inevitability imitate our surroundings.

A child's tendency is to take the easy road and avoid investing the mental energy into their endeavors as do adults. This is precisely the case when it comes to many contemporary Black plays. Recent years have brought a number of these plays, which contain some of the most non-creative and non-provocative writing imaginable. They are reminiscent of the old coon shows of the past. These gospel and/or crude stage plays sweeping through our cities are an embarrassment to Black intellect and have been appropriately labeled as the "Chittlin Circuit." Some examples: *"You Can't Keep A Good Man Down"*; "*Can A Woman Drive A Man Crazy?*"; *"The Diary Of A Black Man";The Diary of a Mad Black Woman"*; "*What A Woman Needs, What A Man Wants"*; *"A Fool in Love"*; *"Lord, All Men Can't Be Dogs*" and *"If These Hips Could Talk*" are only a few of these childishly written *mama who ate the last piece of cornbread* minstrels.

Many of these "plays" possess some of the most elementary, simplistic and predictable dialogue ever written for the stage. People attending these gossip events actually stand up, praise and clap over the most mundane character lines. We react with surprise and excitement over lines, such as "If you lay down with dogs you get up with fleas" or "Honey, you don't need no man with a whole lot of material things. You need a man that's got Jesus in his heart" or "If you don't love me just cuz I put on a few extra pounds, then you never really loved me anyway."

At this point in our social development, why do these redundant and rudimentary lines and cliché's still inspire or impress us? A large percentage of the producers and affiliates of these exhibits are church activists, and it comes blaring through in the stage dialogue.These activists bring with them the predictability and simple-mindedness of the church onto the stage. Quite naturally, the audience is influenced by the customs of the church, and in a similar manner as the church, they praise and shout affirmations to these "plays" that are unmistakably mediocre.

These "plays," like much of the sermonic vocabulary in the Black church, are overly simplistic, crude, unoriginal and lacking in sophistication. Do not, however, associate or confuse sophistication with being bourgeois or uppity. This is a misconception that needs to be eliminated.

Throughout world history, Blacks, regardless of our cultural systems, ritualistic practices or social predicaments, have always displayed intellect, sophistication, morality and class. We have even suffered with a sense of quiet dignity. Today, though, our morality has hit rock bottom in too many of our communities. It seems nothing is sacred anymore. Respect for our bodies, our language, music and relationships are drowning in the cesspools of the secular. Black comedians graphically rape and expose the sacredness of the Black woman. Many Black hip-hop music videos are nothing but soft porn, and a large percentage of the "artists," oddly enough, are wearing big crosses around their necks! Black students ignorantly think studying is a sign of acting White when nothing could be further from the truth.

When we examine the history of Blacks, we are examining a people who are the mothers and fathers of the earth. Blacks once flourished in great African civilizations and are responsible for some of the most spectacular and timeless structures, philosophies, concepts and ideas on earth. Blacks have invented some of the most practical and useful instruments and devices. We have set the standards for higher knowledge, and the whole world has benefited and been influenced by our divine and intelligent contributions.

Blacks could not have once had thriving civilizations, built spectacular pyramids and temples, mastered shipbuilding and agriculture without an extremely high level of intellect and sophistication. At some point during those great times in the past, it is reasonable to assume that Blacks were proactive, practical and understood that success was dependent upon a balance of spirituality *and* intelligence. Like them, our youth should still be aspiring to be great thinkers, philosophers, scientists and inventors, to a larger degree than becoming great athletes and entertainers. We do not need another Black athlete, especially one who lays his millions right back in the laps of his oppressors and exploiters.

The church, ultimately, has to expand its rhetoric and transcend the trappings of tradition by opening itself up to broader possibilities of thought. It is bottled-up rhetoric streaming from the pulpit that limits biblical and other historical research. For instance, why isn't the average church member or so-called Christian, knowledgeable or even curious about the biblical revisions that took place in Europe? It should spark a little interest in us to know that the revisers of the Bible were all non-Black. The often-raised question concerning who wrote the Bible cannot be explained with unresearched answers, simply claiming it was written by "god-inspired" men.

Constantine, one of the most influential figures in Christianity, helped determine what books and passages were to be admitted, omitted and altered in the Bible. Much of the Christian principles on which we stand were actually laws put in place by this Roman Emperor. Constantine, however, was by no means godly. He was a man that had his own son publicly executed and his wife boiled alive!

Other questions in which we should show interest concerns the Council of Nicea. What was it; what took place there; and what role did Constantine play in the shaping of Christianity? Who were those in power at the time the books of the Bible were being written, edited, omitted and retranslated? Who exactly was King James, and why was the Bible revised in the first place? We cannot continue to study a Bible referred to as the King James Version and not know a thing about King James or the historical and political climate during the time Christianity was becoming a major force in the world. We must also question why we, the oldest people on the planet, are studying a *his*-story cloaked in Jewish lineage. Denomination without investigation is foolish, and, it too, is demonstrative of a childlike mindset.

Upon deeper investigation, we will find that the basis of much of our biblical beliefs come directly from the stories of ancient cultures much older than the Bible. The Bible is simply a re-telling of pre-existing myths and legends. Egyptian (African) mythology has had, perhaps, the greatest influence on the Bible. Noted historian Gerald Massey found 137 similarities between the Egyptian Horus and the Christian Jesus, whose story came along thousands of years later. Not only does the life of Horus as documented by ancient texts, hieroglyphics, and respected scholars and historians around the world, confirm that the story of Jesus greatly parallels the Egyptian god, but Mary, the mother of Jesus is an adaptation of the Egyptian goddess Isis. There are far too many similarities and exactitudes between these and many other Egyptian spiritual figures and the characters within the Bible.

Do not consider this blasphemous. This is only information that is not hidden but widely available. The reason a great majority of Blacks do not know this may be due to the fact that we have been conditioned to be mentally lazy. We have grown comfortable with familiar sermonic rhetoric and are, perhaps, too afraid to venture outside of Biblical boundaries that may cause us to act upon our discoveries. We are afraid we will discover something historically plausible that might cause us to exert mental energy in the direction of change. It is often easier to consider new information blasphemous or even bluntly reject it. Being closed minded is like remaining as mental larvae, allowing fear to prevent us from becoming butterflies. We cannot afford to have a "The Bible said it, I believe it and that's all there is to it" approach to knowledge.

If one were to snatch away the sheet music of a classical musician during a performance, he or she would be lost and have difficulty continuing with the piece. Similarly, if one were to take the Bible away from a Black Christian who bases their spiritual knowledge strictly on the Bible, he or she may have trouble elaborating on religious, spiritual and historical matters. How much, based on their own research would they know? I refer to those who cannot elaborate on spiritual matters without continuous reference to the Bible as "*Biblesaysites*."

We must ask questions no matter how painful they seem. Jewish author Gary Greenberg, in his book entitled *The Moses Mystery: The African Origin of the Jewish People,* is courageous enough to ask things that question his own Jewish story. Greenberg asks the questions:

> How do we know, independent of the Bible, that Israel's presence in Egypt was preceded by an earlier presence in Palestine?
>
> Why is there no archaeological record of Israel or the Hebrew people prior to the thirteenth century B.C.? (The period of the so-called biblical Exodus).
>
> Why is there no extrabiblical evidence linking any specific Semitic tribes to the Hebrew people?
>
> And why did the so-called ten lost tribes disappear without an archaeological trace of their existence?

We cannot allow the cliché "If you want to keep something from the Black man, put it in a book" (other than the Bible) to continue to be perceived as true. We have to dig deep and ask questions concerning our beliefs and practices without regarding our natural curiosities as blasphemy.

Also, the congregants in the church profess to be "believers." Belief in something connotes partial conviction because of its inference of doubt. If someone had a diamond in one of their fists and asked us which fist we *believe* the diamond to be in, we would have to guess because we really do not *know*. When we profess to be "believers" in God, it is like saying we really do not know. Knowing can be more potent than believing. We have nothing less to lose by *knowing* something than we have *believing* in something. How many of us would say we are not sure and we really do not *know* Jesus, but we *believe* in Jesus. Essentially, that is what we infer when we call ourselves *believers*. In the book entitled *How to Know God,* by Deepak Chopra, there is a quotation by Simon Weil that states, "What concerns divine things, belief is not appropriate. Only certainty will do. Anything less than certainty is unworthy of God."

Churchgoers will predictably explain that it is all about faith and "Faith is the substance of things hoped for; the evidence of things not seen" (Hebrew 11:1). If faith requires no proof, then imagination becomes the great thing. If we were told to have faith in an almighty polka dot monkey, how could anyone dispute such an idea, especially since we do not have to provide any evidence of the monkey's existence?

Faith is not only associated with religion. One can have faith that the wheels on their car won't fall off when they are riding. We have faith that mechanical and physical laws of nature will continue to serve us.

We give power to that which we focus our energy on. This is precisely the reason there are thousands of religions and belief systems in the world. Many of these "beliefs" are based on mythology, which is simply a timeless expression of the human imagination. People, places and things are "real" if we believe them to be. This is not implying that God is a myth, but those who think mythology does not play a significant role in nearly all of the world's religions, including Christianity, are highly misinformed.

Upsetting traditional dogma may cause discomfort to

many people. It may shake the very foundations upon which their belief system so comfortably rests. One of the reasons we find it difficult to break the chains of rhetorical confinement is fear. Change can be a most frightening undertaking because it forces us to have encounters with traditions.

If what we claim to believe is true and we are confident in that belief, leave it for a while. If it is really true, then nothing else can threaten you. There is nothing to lose.

Being open to new ideas, new avenues of thought, removing our curiosity shackles and brain muzzles, researching and exploring deeper waters, can be rewarding. Never take the position that it is better *not* to know than it is to know. If in fact, we search out grounds beyond the confines of our church doctrines, and find that it is in total contradiction to what we currently have been taught, do not fear the information: face it; accept it; be grateful for it. As Ralph Waldo Emerson stated, "There is no knowledge that is not power."

We must not be afraid to question religious dogma. There are many sources other than religion from which we can learn or be spiritually inspired. We cannot allow the factor of fear to inhibit our growth. Fear is exploitable, and subtly inducing it is one of the most seductive aspects of the Black church. Preachers routinely make implicit "God's gonna get you" types of remarks when we start to question tired, irrelevant, repetitive or sensational sermonic rhetoric. We cannot allow our growth to be hindered by fear, living our lives with the worry of being punished by God. Sermonic rhetoric has helped to instill this trepidation in Blacks. We cannot function properly in society when fear is planted within our conscious.

The Church (Christianity) has been able to successfully recruit and convert people mainly by making them afraid. The editors of the Bible and the establishers of much of our current beliefs have done a masterful job at terrifying people with a patriarchal, monotheistic, authoritarian, dictating and demanding God. The Bible consistently advises us to be afraid and to live in fear. Ecclesiastes 12:13 reads: "Fear God, and keep His commandments." In Luke 12:5 we find the verse: "Fear Him, which after He hath killed hath power to cast into hell; yea, I say unto you, Fear Him." Psalms 128 states: "Blessed is everyone that feareth the Lord."

Many people are intimidated by authority. Authority can be seen as any person, group, system or institution that has the power to enforce, control, manipulate or influence our circumstances. Among us are those who may have once been accused of committing a crime. If so, they have experienced the fear, nervousness and anxiety prior to a scheduled appearance in court. After the court date is announced, we live in a state of fear and uneasiness.

It is surprising to find that much of our religious belief system and the judicial court system have many parallels, due, in large part, to them operating under many of the same anxiety inducing principles.

In the judicial process, for instance, one is accused of a crime. In the religious process, one is born into sin (accused of a crime). In the judicial process one's criminal case receives a trial, and the prosecutor will try to get the judge to send the accused criminal to jail. In the religious process, our lives are constantly on trial to be good, get saved, stay in the Word and avoid sin. The devil is the prosecutor trying to get the judge (God) to send us to hell.

The judicial process establishes a date as to when the judge will render a sentence determining whether the accused criminal will be set free or go to jail. The accused criminal may be offered a chance to speak before the verdict is rendered. The religious process establishes a date after death, our judgment day, when God (the judge) will look back on our lives and may hear our pleas (final remarks), and then render a judgment that will determine whether or not we will go to heaven or hell (our sentence).

It is very unhealthy and unproductive for us to live our lives in fear and as if it were on trial. There must be a total revamping of the way we are currently "sermonized." When we commit crimes or wrongdoings against our fellow human beings, our punishment or sentence is served in the now, not in the hereafter. Our lives are mirrors of our thoughts. What we do and what we think in the now is reflected in the present.

Black preachers are known for encouraging congregations to continuously give praise and thanks to God/Jesus. They tell the people to "Praise Him in the morning when you wake up";"Praise Him on the way to work";"Praise Him while you're eating lunch"; "Praise Him on the way home from work;" and "Praise Him before you go to bed at night." In my opinion, this is a fanatical approach to spirituality and exemplifies religious extremism. An Ethiopian proverb states "Singing Hallelujah everywhere does not prove piety." This is also another form of fear because many Christians who take this approach to worshipping apparently believe it will better their lives in some aspect or perhaps help to insulate them from life's many adversities. If that is true, then we can reason that if they do not consume their days and nights giving praise and thanks to God/Jesus, then they apparently fear their lives will be worsened or more susceptible to life's adversities. Many of us speak of God/Jesus all day, carry Bibles in our cars and constantly listen to gospel music because of a fear that our lives will not be as blessed if we do not do these things.

In the book by Don Miguel Ruiz entitled *Beyond Fear,* he eloquently explains the negative impact of fear.

> Fear is the root of the reality we usually perceive around us. Fear is the source of disease, of war, and

> of alienation from the joy that is our birthright. Fear is the source of all the negative agreements we've made with life.

Blacks are no strangers when it comes to living in fear. We have experienced it in the form of slavery, oppression, intimidation, etc. The worst thing Black folks need is to live in a fear, induced by the teachings of the church.

A marketing book, *Secrets from the Lost Art of Common Sense Marketing,* by H. Brad and Alan J. Antin, presents marketing strategies designed to enhance the sales of whatever products or services a business provides. The book states that a business needs an S.O.B. (Statement of Benefit): the statement, slogan or catch phrase that sets a business apart from the rest of those promoting similar products or services. It tells the consumer why they will benefit from doing business with their company and what they can provide that the others cannot. It is a statement that details the unique aspects of the business.

This idea relates to the church because despite whatever else it may be, it is also a business that needs "sales" to operate. One thing that has helped the church remain in business for so long is the biblical promise (statement of benefit) of a heaven for the righteous. Without the promise of a heaven, the church could not be sold to as many people.

A great number of people were never really churchgoers

in their youth, but as they grew older, they began to faithfully attend. They sense their time on earth shortening and have an urgency to get "right" with God. People who fit this description are often motivated by fear. It is a deep-seated fear of being sent to a lake of fire and burning forever.

The truth of the matter is that many people attend church because they are afraid not to. They are afraid of the consequences of not going. They fear God's wrath and a one-way trip to hell when they die.

Illustration 1

Notice the picture on the billboard in illustration 1. This large, very noticeable advertisement, located outside of Atlanta, is a direct threat and warning to all non-believers, non-Christians or those who may not adhere to such radical, religious dogma. The message is an extreme ultimatum that is offensive to some and fearful to others.

The fear factor is an important element in maintaining the business of the Black church. If no one feared any retribution, church attendance would be greatly affected. Being afraid not to attend church is a perverted way of exercising one's spirituality.

So what does fear have to do with sermons being in a state of rhetorical confinement? In the Black church there are two opposite ends of the sermonic spectrum: heaven and hell. All sermonic roads, no matter which way traveled, ultimately lead to an end point of either eternal damnation (hell) or everlasting life (heaven). They are the two potential destination points where in common belief, we will spend eternity.

Because the Black experience in America has been so ensnared in struggle, the prospect of going to heaven has always been very appealing. The very idea of being in a place where there would be no more suffering, heartache, pain, misery or racism seems too irresistible not to keep that idea in the forefront of church doctrine. Having faith in a utopian world beyond this problematic, present day world, has been a psychological gift for Blacks.

The underlying theme of most sermons is *ultimately* about how to make it to heaven and how to avoid hell when we die. This central concept is the sun that mostly all sermons orbit around. It is the ultimate goal of believers. If the preacher does not drift outside of that orbit, the rhetorical scenery will not change much. Unless you develop on the theme, you cannot significantly develop on the rhetoric. It is similar to a song that has a very basic and simple theme or chorus and never changes its key, tempo or chord pattern. In this case, there is not much one can do to make the song more interesting, which is one of the reasons why so many preachers constantly struggle to find material to preach about on Sunday morning.

If the theological concept and sermonic language are underdeveloped, it will be difficult for the people to develop. That may be the primary reason many churches do not encourage much expansion of thought (independent of the Bible). When the people's thoughts expand, the sermonic scenery will be forced to change.

Preachers often ride or camouflage their best "horses" (slang for a sermon that has been around the track a few times) hoping we won't recognize it, have forgotten it or have never heard it.

In his book *Pulpit Confessions: Exposing The Black Church*, N. Moore lists the many scandalous things a great number of Black preachers do when they run out of sermons. The book states that preachers are known to go to libraries, copy sermons and even tear pages right out of books and preach those exact sermons.They shamelessly plagiarize for a living, stealing sermons from a variety of sources and use them as their own. Moore disclosed how some will preach, verbatim, sermons at 10a.m. based on those they heard on the radio earlier that morning! In addition, at revivals, Moore, an ex-preacher, revealed how preachers commonly peddle off typed, reheated sermons to the highest bidder.

In changing times, it is unrealistic for us to hear the same trite sermonic rhetoric generation after generation and expect to have different results.

Another rhetorical trick preachers keep in their hip pockets and use as bread and butter sermons, is a technique I call sin-sationalization. Whenever the well of sermons runs dry, preachers can always re-wet the spirits of the congregation by conveniently creating stark contrasts between those who are perceived as sinners and those who are perceived as righteous.

Sin-sationalization sermons play upon the minds of congregations and are good for reinforcing the idea that everyone should be in church. For instance, preachers will make sharp distinctions between the "sinful and wicked" people of the world, and the "true and righteous." They often create the greatest wedges among us. Preachers present a bleak portrait of those who are so-called "in the world" (non-churchgoers). Preachers then paint biased pictures that depict rosier realities of those that faithfully attend church. Those attending the church instantly feel good because they are not perceived as sinners and feel more favorable in God's eye. They see themselves as remotely different in contrast to the world of "sinners." The congregation thus responds with affirmative reactions, praises and testimonials based on their perceived favorableness with God. This scare tactic is a sure-fire way to assure them that they are in the right place and on the path to heaven.

The importance of being in church is further emphasized in the book *Adam! Where Are You?:Why Most Black Men Don't Go to Church* by Jawanza Kunjufu. Kunjufu states that 95% of African American male inmates did not attend church. However, there is another way of interpreting this statistic. Maybe they did not attend because it lacked the substance needed to connect with them. Although their actions are dictated by choice, Black drug dealers and thieves are also returns on generations of impotent sermonic investments. These same "sinners" that preachers refer to are the direct descendants of those Blacks who were part of a time when the vast majority of us were active in the church. What powerful spiritual message was passed down to the youth?

The rhetoric that flows from the pulpit places a great emphasis on a time to come. The church has been an institution largely predicated upon a future reward and heavily rooted in the soil of the supernatural. This doctrine of waiting does not appeal to a young generation geared toward immediate gratification. To many youth, preachers often lack concreteness, and the church is regarded as a feel good place that does not speak directly to their specific and practical needs, such as money, respect, reputation and peer pressure. Many churches do have programs that address these particular needs and should be applauded, but there are some that require membership before these services can be used.

Following the September 11th World Trade Center attack, there was a slight increase in youth attendance. Unfortunately, fear and uncertainty were the motivating factors. Church represented an emotional safety valve for many people. Many followers of traditional, mainstream preachers were once again jumping on the familiar apocalyptic bandwagon. Countless people ran around proclaiming that "Jesus was coming back."

In some countries, men, women and children are constantly engaged in war and live with terrorism and its threat everyday. Where are the cries of "Jesus is coming back" on their behalf? Is God, the proclaimed creator of all people, only going to intervene in man's affairs when the United States gets into a crisis?

Thousands of churches throughout the United States (Black and White) joined the "God Bless America" crusade, plastering the slogan all over their street display signs. From a spiritual perspective, wouldn't it be more appropriate, especially coming from the church, to display "God Bless the *World*?"

Whenever a national calamity occurs, many opportunistic "Armageddonites" begin declaring that the world is coming to an end. During the Y2K scare they reemerged on the scene to advocate their end of the world campaign.

So, as usual, September 11th brought its share of insecurity and apocalyptic entrepreneurs. Preachers took major advantage of and greatly capitalized on the people's paranoia. They made tons of money in the process. Church attendance increased 24% the two weeks following September 11th. When bombing began in Iraq only 18 months after September 11th, fear and uncertainty spread throughout the nation once again. Ironically, gun sales also skyrocketed. In other words, praise the Lord and pass the ammunition.

Tragedies as well as holidays, in a financial sense, are beneficial for preachers. Easter Sunday, for example, is a day when Blacks flock to church in droves flaunting new hats, shoes, purses and suits that we have been exploited (tricked) into buying. We tithe to our heart's delight and are filled with a good soul-grabbing sermon, usually about the story of Calvary and how Jesus rose on the third day. Come Monday morning we are faced with less money, while the clothing outlets and manufacturers deposit our money into banks outside of our communities. And the next time Easter Sunday rolls around, masses of Blacks will repeat these same steps, keeping to the same mental trajectory until they radically alter their way of thinking.

Isaac Newton's first law of motion states: Every object in a state of uniform motion tends to remain in that state of motion unless an external force is applied to it. Blacks, in a sense, are in a state of uniform motion (mental trajectory), and we are in need of an external force (change, and enlightenment) to redirect our path.

Whenever there is a spiritual gathering of people, preachers must take advantage of this valuable time because words are precious, cannot be squandered nor the people's time taken for granted. Their language has to be effective enough to institute change.

3 Privation Rationalization

He who is unable to dance says that the yard is stony.
– Kenyan Proverb

One of the most enduring paradoxes of the Black church is that many sermons address the need for us to increase (prosper), yet there is a subtle nurturing of privation tolerance and rationale. Webster's Dictionary defines privation as: *deprivation, the loss or absence of some quality or condition. Privation is the state of being without; the act of depriving somebody of something.*

On one hand, there is a lot of preaching on how we can improve the quality and conditions of our lives, but on the other we have been conditioned, theologically, to accept our being without. We have been indoctrinated with the idea that despite our levels of deprivation the most important thing in our lives is to be in God's good favor and to have Jesus Christ as our personal savior. Preachers comfort their congregations by reassuring them that this old sinful world will soon come to an end anyway.

They have conditioned their congregations with the biblical passage taken from the book of Matthew 19:30, which reads: But many that are first shall be last; and the last shall be first. Because the Black experience in America has been one filled with deprivation, preachers have used this biblical passage to encourage us not to worry if we are deprived (last) because in the end we will finish first.

Privation rationalization among African Americans naturally evolved from the result of our experience in America. Because of the futile reality of slavery, Blacks were forced to use the power of hope and faith as coping devices. There was a psychological need to believe that one day a Messiah would intervene and radically change our fate. For Blacks, there were many times when tolerating privation has not been an option. There have also been times when rationalizing privation has been psychologically mandatory.

Blacks were enslaved and physically confined to plantations with no concrete indications of when or if freedom would come. Rationalizing their condition was a necessary tactic for psychological preservation. It was incumbent upon them to find coping and ego defense mechanisms, or a spiritual death was inevitable. They could not turn to America for help, but could turn to Jesus. Christianity thus became the comforter in which to wrap themselves.

According to the book *African American Religion*, edited by Timothy E. Fulop & Albert J. Raboteau, most Africans who were brought to the English colonies had not been Christians in their homeland.The book goes on to say that significant Christianization of Blacks did not begin until after 1760, and even more significantly, after 1830 when most were native born. They found the teachings of Christianity appealing because it indoctrinated them with the idea that even though they were enslaved, as long as they believed in Jesus, one day all of their suffering would be over. Because of our unique past, many of us still have the mindset that fosters privation tolerance and rationalization.

One blistering winter day while living in Cleveland, Ohio, I drove downtown during my lunch hour. As I pulled over to park in front of a fast food establishment, I noticed a middle-aged African American woman scavenging through an industrial-sized garbage dumpster. She pulled out what appeared to be a small sandwich and began methodically eating, picking the food apart until it completely disappeared.

This disturbed me tremendously, and I felt the need to do something to help her. I went inside the restaurant and bought her a sandwich, fries and a hot chocolate. I approached the lady with a smile and offered her the food. She accepted it with a little trepidation. I asked her in a roundabout, but respectable way, how she had become reduced to such conditions and what was she doing to help herself. She seemed relatively sane but a little hesitant and unwilling to go into detail about her predicament. She turned to me, as she wiped her mouth with her coat sleeve, and said with a confident grin, "I'm okay, as long as I've got Jesus." Now, that is an extreme example of privation rationale, but more common examples are all around us.

Many Blacks have been programmed to accept less (including less knowledge) and even rationalize their sub-standard living conditions. Countless Black people have said, "I might not be rich or have any power, but I've got my health. God woke me up this morning, and I can see, I can walk, and I'm in my right frame of mind." This is a wonderful approach for life but not for living. We have adopted an "It could be worse" attitude toward life. This approach will only assure cultural subordination, and we will wind up becoming functional inferiors. We have to expect more from ourselves and see ourselves as godlike; worthy to receive the highest heights of what life has to offer.

There is twisted irony in the sense of privation being a prerequisite to prosperity. The church is a storehouse of testimonials and songs that follow the classic pattern of being "down and out with nowhere to turn" prior to finding the Lord "who changed my life around." There is always the ever-present storm before the calm. "I was *lost* but now I'm found"; "We *fall down* but we get up"; "I was *blind* but now I see"; "I was *in danger* of the hell-fire, but now I have eternal salvation"; "I once made my *home in the streets*, but now my home is in the house of the Lord"; and "My *bills were behind*, and I had nowhere to go and then the Lord poured me out a blessing." These are only a few examples of the negative before the positive, the low before the high, and the privation before the prosperity scenarios.

Life's pattern, however, is not always so inclined. Certainly, we all have problems and mountains to climb—there are no exceptions. We as a people, though, have got to stop memorializing our problems. We hold them up high. We tend to "worship" our trying experiences and see them as nobilities, while showing off our battle scars in the process. They also give us things about which to testify. Preachers construct verbal monuments in recognition of our problems. It is almost as if we enjoy being the victim and the underdog so that we can have a reason to keep our cycles of Sunday sermons spinning. We hold onto our tribulations like they were lottery tickets and then cash them in emotionally at church.

Black preachers need to be careful not to make privation appear as a prerequisite to prosperity. People will not fight for what they are convinced they already have. By the same token, people will fight for what they are convinced they do not have.

When folks testify about how lost, down or deprived they were until they found God, it does not tell the whole story about the work *they* inevitably had to do. It does not speak of the sacrifices they made or the discipline they exhibited that helped them elevate from their previous conditions. In the book of James 2:14 it reads: What doth it profit, my brethren, though a man say he hath faith, and have not works?

For generations, Black preachers have intoxicated their congregations with rhetoric that says (especially without Jesus) they are so poor, lost, weak, without and blind, even though most of us do not fit these pitiful descriptions. The preacher is feeding us a plate of self-powerlessness. This kind of indoctrination hardens into belief systems and eventually become self-fulfilling realities.

We perceive Jesus as being on our side. Maybe this is because he is presented to us as being a light for those in darkness and a resuscitator for the dead. It is easy to see why Jesus is mostly appealing to the underclass, the poor, minorities, victims and the oppressed. Black people, because of past experiences and classic sermonic indoctrination, perceive themselves (consciously or unconsciously) as possessing all of the aforementioned negative qualities. Jesus is viewed as a champion for the underdog, or those that perceive themselves as such (a vast majority of Blacks).

When we excessively associate Jesus as a healer for the sick, and he is the essence of our worshipping experience, aren't we implying that we are sick, victims, underdogs, blind and lost? If we adhere to the fundamental teachings of Christianity, we follow the belief that we are born into sin and are ill until Jesus heals us. When we subscribe to the idea that we are sick, we will always keep going to the hospital (church), seeking psychiatric treatment from our doctors (preachers).

We often say or have heard things said such as "Lord, you said it wouldn't be easy, and the roads would be rocky." Because of our sermonic orientation, everything seems to center around overcoming hurt, pain and privation. Preachers benefit when we perceive ourselves as prey. This keeps us flocking back to church, where it's safe from the illusion of predators. Jesus is envisaged to work endlessly, elevating us from a *lower* to a *higher* state. We make the mistake by starting from a premise that denies our innate divinity. Our inner thermostats that regulate how we perceive ourselves are automatically defaulted to low. When we begin with a premise based on *self*-denial, we make ourselves vulnerable to being manipulated by religious dogma.

Blacks are unique, in the sense that we do not think highly of ourselves. We refer to ourselves as "niggas" (a self-demotion), devalue our coarser hair textures and degrade each other's skin tones. In addition to these mentally ill attributes, the church has conditioned us to see ourselves as lowly, unworthy sinners in desperate need of cleansing, healing and saving. Many of our gospel songs support this theological concept. The popular song entitled *Too Close To The Mirror* is one of many examples of how Blacks have been classically programmed to minimize their deeds and see the magnitude of their being through a peephole. The hook to this much beloved song is as follows:

Not anything
I've done Lord,
As far as I can see,
Guess I'm too close
To the mirror
To see what you
See in me.

Lyrics such as these are typical. As humble as they may be, they are reflective of an oppressive and racist system. Through overt tactics and the more implicit means of mass media, our conquerors have attempted to sell us on the idea that we are intellectually, aesthetically and divinely subordinate.

During slavery, suffering was monumental. Preachers on

plantations naturally targeted their sermons to the victim. Today's preachers are living and breathing vestiges of that plantation consciousness. This is precisely why the language of many preachers still caters to the causes of the victim (the mentally enslaved). We are a people sick with victimization syndrome and the preacher is the primary perpetuator of this disease because in addition to being preachers, they are also "victimologists." They too, have been inoculated with the same theosophical idealism as the rest of us. It is a case of the blind leading the blind. Preachers bring attention to our down times, and like magicians, get us to think along the wrong grooves by applying the art of misdirection. They are masters at creating the illusion that we are down, and they are lifting us up.

Because sermons concentrate on finding ways to alleviate suffering and continuously revolve around avoiding pain, suffering becomes the object of our fears. We are terrified of being subjected to the type of suffering we once experienced, which is why we become so emotionally grateful whenever "God" enables us to avoid pain or rise from our degradation. This preoccupation with suffering and all of its byproducts can sometimes manifest itself into extensions of our imaginations. Our pain is sometimes real and sometimes imagined. If we perceive ourselves as victims, then we will be victims. Because of this poor-man conditioning, the Black collective perception tends to be on a crawling-out-from-under-existence, and we do not realize that much of the time we are crawling out from under our own self-created delusions.

When we consider how we were brought to this and other countries as kidnapped Africans, chained and shackled by inhumane, profit seeking vultures, it is a travesty that the victims sang and embraced songs such as *Amazing Grace*, which says,

> Amazing Grace!
> How sweet the sound
> That saved a
> wretch like me.
> I once was lost
> But now I'm found,
> Was blind but now I see.

What is amazing is that humble, innocent people were made to believe *they* were wretches! *Amazing Grace* is a song that most appropriately describes its author, John Newton, a slave owner (a lost, blind wretch) who allegedly found God.

Richard X. Donovan clearly states in the book *Black Scientists of America* :

> Life is very much what we choose to emphasize. It is easy for some to emphasize the difficulties and the obstacles. Others may emphasize the opportunity and the challenge. Success is almost beyond reach unless a person emphasizes opportunity. Although chance cannot be ignored, it is primarily a matter of choice.

Many nutritional experts say you should never go to the grocery store when you are hungry because you will be motivated to buy more food. One can think of the church as a grocery store. Preachers spend time convincing us that we are lacking much, so we can come to church hungry. We will then be motivated to buy more of the sermonic rhetoric that conditions us with how lost, blind and weak we are.

When a person is down and out and on their last leg, there is a plethora of resources, in addition to the church, to help them overcome. School, meditation, fasting, money, exercise, attitude and diet are a few important things that can help bring about positive changes in our lives. We should look upon the church as *one* source of inspiration, not the only source. The presence of God is carried within you at all times and in all that you do.

There is a beautiful woman, in her late fifties or early sixties, who lives in California. During her prime years, her husband was an alcoholic, a reckless gambler and physically abusive. Now that she is older, she ponders, in retrospect how sheltered her life has been and realizes the many places and things she never got to see or do. With her husband's health failing and the two managing on a limited income, she now finds herself completely immersed in the church. At this point in her life she feels that the church can somehow redeem her of a life filled with deprivation.

Maybe the church can offer her some solace, but I wonder if she would be so engulfed in the church had her past life been more fulfilling. She, it seems, has learned to submit and rationalize her current state of unhappiness as have many Black women.

Many pastors counsel Black women directly or imply through sermonic rhetoric that it is all right to be without a man as long as they have Jesus. These sentiments are subliminally supported in gospel music. For instance, when we examine the lyrics in gospel music (excluding words such as savior, Jesus, Father, God, etc.), we find they are very similar to R&B or soul music. When women sing R&B or soul music, they sing about the love of a man. When they sing gospel music, they sing about the love of Jesus.

Notice the similarities in the lyrics (language) of gospel songs that are also found in many popular R&B or soul songs: "You are more precious than gold"; "You made my life complete"; "You made me whole again"; "You are all I need"; "You are my joy"; and "Can't nobody love me like you." Perhaps, the lyrics in gospel music that sound similar to those in R&B or soul music, vicariously satisfies the soul of Black women with respect to her needs to deeply love a man.

One gospel song stated it this way: "I'm in love with a man, and his name is Jesus." Because of our lyrics (language) and the fact that the availability of Black males is diminishing, many women are becoming comfortable with the idea that Jesus is the only man they need. This notion sometimes serves as an ego defense mechanism that helps them cope with the reality of not having a man. The love of Jesus and the love of a boyfriend are certainly not the same kind of love. We are speaking, however, on the practical kind of love only a natural man can provide.

In the magazine *Gospel Today*, an article entitled "Single & Successful Living God's Way," Cheryl Martin, former host of Black Entertainment Television, encourages Black women to be "single, satisfied and successful—God's way." Martin states that it is a myth that a woman needs a man to be satisfied and states further that a woman should pursue God first and not a man.

It is true that a woman's success should not measured by whether or not she has a man. It is also possible for a woman to be satisfied without having a man in her life. We have to be careful, though, not to turn single Black women into single, rationalizing Black women. To offer encouragement to those that are single is one thing. To encourage them to be single is quite another.

Adopting the attitude that Jesus is "all you need" with regards to a man is an irrational, and impractical form of rationalization. When women rationalize about not having a man, it can limit their efforts when it comes to searching or making themselves accessible to one. Sitting back and waiting for God to send you a man is no different from the Black collective sitting back and waiting for other miracles to effect change.

If you want to pray for a mountain to move, then pray for a shovel. Do not just pray the mountain will be moved. In other words, change comes from our efforts. It may indeed be all right for a woman to be without a man, but no privation of any kind should be acceptable "as long as you have Jesus." Those are dangerous seeds to scatter because they germinate into fruits of impracticality.

4 Ritualistic Suspension

It takes a deep commitment to change and an even deeper commitment to grow.
– Ralph Ellison

One of the ways the church has helped to limit Black progress has to do with its inability to recognize the need for change. Regression tends to be valued over progression. This is understandable when we consider the fact that the church has been one of the most effective painkillers for Black suffering. It is a difficult challenge for the church to abandon certain customs, theosophical ideas, rituals and modes of conduct. Historically, in this country, Blacks have been in a constant state of overcoming. There have been times when the only true place of refuge was the church. We possessed limited resources and could not call upon the government, courts, police, media, etc., but could always depend on the church. Whether it was an anti-slavery or Civil Rights Movement, the church was the place where we conceived some of our most important ideas.

Although the institution of the church and the doctrine of faith it provided has been an inspiration to Blacks during their lowest times, we must now accept the fact that our world has dramatically changed. We, of course, still have our share of societal problems, but to a greater degree than that of the past, our problems are more self-imposed. There has always been and always will be racism in America, but Blacks today have more choices, more mobility and more access to information.

Black preachers must learn to evolve and adjust to the changing times. They must reevaluate their preaching styles, especially as it relates to their theatrical and emotional conduct behind the pulpit. Our roles and positions in society have changed. Blacks, as a whole, must determine the relevance of the many rituals, customs and traditions of the church, many of which originated from places we are not aware.

Most of us were required to attend church as children. We participated in the rituals without question and have continued as adults to acquiesce to the church's traditions and systems of worship. Numerous customs, rituals and preaching styles were inventions of necessity. They were pertinent for the times out of which they evolved and were indicative of where we were mentally as a unit. But have our traditions, rituals, emotional approaches, religious or spiritual concepts, etc., in today's times, outgrown their usefulness?

The church emerged during a time when Blacks were disenfranchised, terrorized and mistreated on all levels. Although we have never truly reached the equality promised, we are light years away from the conditions that existed during the Black church's inception. Today, we have freedoms previously unimagined. We live in better neighborhoods, have better paying jobs and wear designer clothing more than any other group. In other words, we are no longer in that "Lawd Hamurcy" consciousness the church still perpetuates.

Generally speaking, our hurdles are not necessarily greater than other people of color around the world. Shoutin', whoopin', praisin', testifyin' and feel good Sunday sermons will certainly not resolve the problems we have. It is going to take application, logic, sophistication, intelligence, strategy and a theological rhetoric that incorporates pragmatism and utilitarianism. Our collective problems will not be prayed away. They will only be resolved by making smarter adjustments to the way we think.

"Southern fried chicken" preaching served its purpose, but in today's complex world, that style is a relic; an old cobwebbed mode that has lost its power to bring about real holistic and tangible change. Preachers have to move out of the shouting age and into one that encourages congregations to engage in critical thinking.

There are certain traditions and styles Black preachers must rid themselves of, especially when those particular ways lose their effectiveness. Just because we have been doing something for a long time does not mean we are powerless to change it.

The church is in a state of ritualistic suspension. Every Sunday at church there are specific protocols, rituals and procedural steps that are part of the service. Eventually, it leads to the main event—the sermon. Just like denomination without investigation is rampant among Black believers, so are rituals without reason. In some church services, the rituals sometimes take on more significance than the actual sermons.

We have to be mindful of the current customs and common styles of many of today's preachers. They are rooted in the old plantation Negro style of preaching. Vestiges of these styles and rituals are the repetitiveness, shouting, altar calls, whooping and stage animation. Blacks began to embody the emotional styles of preaching during the Second Great Awakening in the early 19th century. This is when the emotional fervor of the evangelical forms of Protestantism began to sweep through southern plantations.

It is important to realize that this manner of preaching also evolved out of an existence under great duress. Blacks, who were consistently beaten, physically and mentally detained, sold and subjected to physical labor unfit for humans, were not operating on all mental cylinders. This screaming, pacing, handkerchief-head-wiping and underdeveloped style of preaching evolved out of an enslaved mentality. The ensuing mentality became a reactionary response related to what was coerced upon us by our conquerors.

Black preachers are still unconsciously preaching out the horrors of slavery. This is called post-traumatic slave syndrome. We are operating as the end products of inhumanity. The suffering we have endured in this country was previously unknown to the world. Slavery had always existed, but what made the Black Trans-Atlantic slave trade so unique was its dehumanizing aspect. It was an attempt by slave owners to make Blacks hate every facet of themselves through a demoralizing litany of whitewashing.

When we create rituals or patterns of church behavior born out of our own experiences, without any external influences, we are less susceptible to being the predictable pawns of society. The patterns of societal pawns can not only be predicted, but manipulated as well. Two of the worst attributes to have as a people are predictability and manipulability. It is dangerous for others to know what we will do before we do it. It is also a sad commentary on behalf of African Americans for others to know where a great majority of us will be on

Sunday morning, know we will vote Democrat, or know that if they supply our communities with drugs or guns, we will use and abuse them. Hollywood knows we will buy half of all movie tickets, and certain industries know we will flock toward name brand apparel. Car rim manufacturers know they can count on us to help make them wealthy.

Our collective mental pulse begins at the pulpit. As the rhetoric and rituals behind the pulpit changes, the people will change also. The church has always been the dog that wags the tail (the people). If it is in a non-progressive state, still clinging to ill-suited traditions and we attend church in droves, consequentially this will limit our collective growth and development.

New times call for new thoughts, and ultimately new thoughts will lead to new actions. There is a changing political climate that is priming the inhabitants of the earth for a "New World Order." There is a need to adjust to these changing times. Blacks have begun this century with retrograde rituals. We must develop a different theosophical vocabulary while incorporating church rituals that are more conducive to the times.

Another old sermonic filler (ritual) that has been conditioned into the Black consciousness is our concept of the devil. Black preachers are notorious for indoctrinating their congregations with the idea of an ever-present devil in our midst, relentlessly trying to destroy our lives in every conceivable way. It is very convenient to assign blame to a devil and attribute most of our problems to this evil while absolving ourselves of any responsibility in the process. As long as there is a devil in the picture, the preacher has somebody to shout about on Sunday morning. Whenever there is a bad guy, there is a story to be told and a potential victory to be won. Preachers use the devil in the church as target practice to show off their sermonic marksmanship. They invite the devil into their sermons because it allows them the opportunity to throw "him" out of it. If we were told that we, and we alone, were responsible for our own successes and failures, the preacher would not have much of an opportunity to be our hero.

Whenever we are sick, unemployed, broke, afraid, divorcing, etc., we attribute these things to the devil. When we perceive the devil in such a way, it forces us to look, irresponsibly, outside ourselves as the reason for our problems. For instance, if we are financially broke, instead of bringing the devil into it, take into account that perhaps it may be due to a lack of effort, mismanagement of money, inadequate job skills, or a lack of education. Pointing our fingers at a devil provides excuses for our problems. It is an irresponsible approach to spirituality, and, yet, another way of rationalizing our privation.

The concept of a devil being out to get us and being the primary reason for the problems in our lives became widespread during the early establishment of the Christian orthodox movement. The devil was a way of frightening people and making them conform to the church's religious idealism.

A very popular Black preacher's sermon revolved around the idea of "beating the devil." He created an emotional circus by telling the congregation how they were able to defeat the devil. He shouted, "Look back at your lives and say: I don't have cancer anymore. I don't have a lump in my breast anymore. I'm not on drugs anymore. I'm not living in the streets anymore." How many times have we "beaten the devil" and that which was beaten was brought on by us in the first place? We create our own monsters and then later choose to destroy what we created. Of course, we may experience setbacks that are unforeseeable and seemingly beyond our control, but many of our issues are brought on by a set of circumstances *we* initiated. For instance, we may have once been addicted to drugs and then beat the addiction—the "devil." Remember, it was our decision in the first place to use drugs. If we beat the devil by lowering our cholesterol or high blood pressure, it was our actions/eating habits to begin with that contributed to the problem. We are products of our thoughts and choices.

A great book entitled *Think and Grow Rich: A Black*

Choice, by Dennis Kimbro and Napoleon Hill, elaborates on the many reasons we fail and why many negative things happen in our lives. It states that virtually all limitations are self-imposed.

> [Kimbro writes] You will soon realize that you, the individual, as such, you have no limitations except those accepted in your own mind. Every man and woman has within himself or herself a sleeping giant.

Beating the devil should not be the goal of our day or the goal in our lives. Correct thinking beats the "devil" and is what our day should center around. Essentially, we create our own devils. We create them when we use bad judgment, think incorrectly, and make the wrong choices. This devil beating gospel that many preachers utilize to entertain their congregants is a sensationalizing tactic they find very effective. It is so subliminally powerful that congregants who may have never experienced the specific problems their preacher highlights, actually start to believe they have. It is a psychological technique called the power of suggestion; a form of hypnosis whereby the preacher compels us to think, say, or do whatever he chooses. He suggests you have or have had a particular problem, and you subconsciously buy into it. The electrifying emotional atmosphere created by the preacher helps the pill (the suggestion) go down more easily.

Preachers need our perceptions of privation to have something from which to rescue us. They need to save us at the end of their sermons. They need our perceptions of a persistent devil in our midst, so they can have a bad guy to fight with during the sermon. They require the sermonic battle between good and evil in order to come up victorious in the "12th round" of the sermon. Preachers give their congregations "binoculars," so they will see their problems as being bigger than they are. This, in turn, creates monsters for the preacher to wrestle with and gives him opportunities to appear as though he is rescuing (saving) us from something.

Whenever the need for sermonic change arises, preachers must take heed. We cannot continue to be stuck on retro rituals. It may have once been appropriate for them to speak of ever-present devils, preach emotionally exhausting sermons, and sing songs about going to heaven, but we are now in the age of information where we must implement critical thinking and direct spiritual application. We are no longer children fresh out of reconstruction. Many of our rituals have outgrown their usefulness, and we are stuck in a state of ritualistic suspension and sermonic obsolescence. Much the same as a personal computer needs upgrading, so our brain computer and spiritual database need it also.

5 The Need for Relevance

Wood may remain ten years in the water, but it will never become a crocodile.
– Zairean proverb

Many preachers, as stated in chapter 3, teach messages of increase (economic prosperity), but can we really apply these teachings practically? It has to be more than blanket messages, which essentially state that if we obey God's word we will have more and live more abundantly, or if we do the opposite then we will receive the opposite. That may be true, but at some point we have to make investments, save money, budget and keep our emotions separate from our business. Some say the role of the church should not extend into teaching things of this nature. Maybe they're right, but the role of preachers should definitely be more than parading around in expensive suits, getting their egos massaged and telling us things we already inherently or intuitively know.

Because we attend church in droves and with great consistency, its role should be more accountable when disseminating valuable information. For example, it should enlighten us to the correct political candidates that have our best interests at heart. Churches generate money from our communities, which naturally ties them to the Black economy. Preachers should educate us about our local and national spending habits and make an effort to provide community-based and national solutions for empowering the Black economy as a whole. It should be continuously active in informing us of how foolishly we spend our dollars.

It is estimated that African Americans spend 29 billion dollars annually but spend less than five percent of those dollars within the Black community. The church should inform the congregation of where and how tithe money is being utilized. We should be informed of how we are being economically and socially exploited in so many ways. Yes, there are magazines, newspapers, the internet and more, that provide this type of information but, unfortunately, over 50% of the Black population is not gathered in front of computers or reading magazines or newspapers every Sunday morning. Church seems to be the most practical and logical conduit for disseminating pertinent information to the masses of our people.

Blacks, because of our unique past and the racist, oppressive tactics designed to create division among us, have developed a deep mistrust and a low tolerance of disagreement toward one another. We are severely lacking a consolidated stance on anything collectively beneficial. What is it we see or perceive when we are face to face with one another? Do we simply see a beautiful and divine Black person who is a descendant of the mothers and fathers of the world? Or, on the other hand, do we focus on all of the insignificant peripheral aspects of each other such as what we are wearing, what we are driving, where we are living, or what we do for a living?

There is such a great deal of ideological and theological fragmentation amongst Blacks that the very thought of us coming together for a unified cause is almost an oxymoron. But, ironically, in many cities with large Black populations, there are "Black Family Reunions." These are annual weekend gatherings designed to promote unity among Black families and communities.

This indicates there is a pulse beating in the collective consciousness of the Black race. Our colorblind ministries, however, ignore our special needs and unique circumstances. Large national and international Black ministries, as a consequence, have significant White memberships. That is wonderful as an idea, but it probably limits what Black preachers can or cannot address within their sermons. A cliché states: *Stand for something or fall for anything*. When we do not collectively stand for something, we become more susceptible to being exploited (falling for anything).

What do preachers insist that we stand for or commit to as a Black unit (besides Jesus)? The best place to instill a sense of group consciousness is in the church. Blacks must learn to commit to a collective cause. Many of us have heard the statement that "Blacks don't stick together." It is impossible to stick together when we do not have a legitimate agenda.

Black people, though, are in an ongoing affair of stick-to-itiveness when it comes to the Democratic Party. Why is this? The Democratic Party, admittedly, has done its share of good such as initiating programs like Head Start, but should the masses be fully committed to them? Are they dramatically improving our overall conditions? We should be committed to policies, not parties.

As far as the church is concerned, committing ourselves to the principles of Jesus Christ is a very humble and noble thing to do. The parables that he spoke are valuable. How do we make his life relevant so that being "Christ-like" does not translate into being commercially exploited, musically vulgar, predictable, passive, violent and self-eradicating? Our actions are not only counterrevolutionary but counter to all that is worthy of respect. If Black preachers insist on teaching the principles of Jesus, they must make them relevant to Black liberation and empowerment, or we will be in danger of perishing. We are facing the real threat of extinction/obsolescence.

Some churches teach an *Afrocentric* version of the scriptures, in which they inform us that Jesus, Moses, Solomon, Jeremiah, and many more Biblical characters were Black. Afrocentric sermonizing in itself is not sufficient. It does no good to swap the ethnicities of the characters within the Bible but preach the same irrelevancy. The preacher who discovers Afrocentricity within the Bible and makes it *relevant* to the Black cause, will be the preacher who lays the golden egg.

Cultures in ancient societies "created" their deities and made them relevant to their circumstances. Deities and saviors were tailor-made to serve in the interests of the people and their environment. For example, in Egypt, the Sun and the Nile River were both vitally important to the people. These two forces were indispensable and crucial to their existence. The yearly floods of the great Nile River brought forth vegetation and life sustenance. The Sun provided warmth and caused the vegetation to grow. The Egyptian's understanding of the universe was influenced by what they saw around them and what was necessary for their survival. These two essential components of their culture gave rise to the sun god *Re* or *Atum-Re*.The annual flooding, which provided nutrients and fertilization of the land, influenced their concepts of the origin of life.

Blacks must be spiritually motivated by what we see around us. There may be elements within this particular revised (King James Version) Bible that fosters complacency, passiveness, dependency, and an unproductiveness of which we are not conscious, or are able to perceive and decipher. Perhaps we need to do a reinterpretation of scripture, making it more conducive and relative to our specific circumstances. We may have to, in a sense, *flip the script*-ture in a way that is more favorable to our plight. White slave owners flipped the script by interpreting (perverting) certain scriptures to their advantage. In Luke 12:47, the Bible states: And that servant, which knew his Lord's will, and prepared not *himself*, neither did according to his will, shall be beaten with many stripes. The slave masters played this verse to the hilt. They saw scripture through blue eyes and made it work for them.

Ephesians 6:5 reads: *Servants*, be obedient to them that are your masters according to the flesh, with fear and trembling, in singleness of heart, as unto Christ. What a beautiful scripture for the owners of plantations! Although these Biblical scriptures were taken out of context, they served as tools for slave owners. Biased interpretations were used to get the most out of their free Black labor.

Scriptures do not have to be taken totally out of context in order to fit the relevance of our circumstances. It is just a matter of readjusting the way we process the information within our religious texts. Elijah Muhammad, the founder of the Nation of Islam, was a master at making Islam relevant to the specific circumstances of Blacks. He was able to place a necessary Black slant on it without corrupting the religion or its text.

Unfortunately, there are far too many brainwashed Blacks who believe that being pro-Black naturally translates into being anti-something else. One of the most potent remarks concerning the need for Black relevance within the church is found in the book *Our Black Seminarians & Black Clergy Without a Black Theology* by the great educator Yosef A.A. ben-Jochannan (affectionately known as Dr. Ben). Mwalimu Jaramogi Abebe Agyeman, in a passage of the book had this to say:

> We see every aspect of worship in a traditional Black church contributing to Black enslavement. Many Black Christians accept baptism as a mystery by which they are changed in their relationship with God so that they can escape from sin and the problems of life and fly away home. They die to the old sinful life, putting aside petty personal sins such as card playing, drinking, and fornicating. The entire experience has no meaning in terms of the Black Liberation Struggle. In a world in which color determines every aspect of their daily lives, conversion and salvation are considered colorless. They are still going to buy from white stores, vote for white candidates, and straighten their hair in order to look like

> their oppressor. They do not conceive of the Christian church involved in a revolutionary struggle to liberate Black people from the oppression of white people.

The passage continues with the words of the former director of the Center for Urban Black Studies in San Francisco, Dr. W. Hazaiah Williams:

> The Black church only appears to be otherworldly because it defines worldly objectives in heavenly terminology easily translated and understood by Black congregations. I wish that this were true, but a Black congregation hears what a Black preacher says, and only when the framework has been clearly defined in terms of individual salvation are they willing to ride the waves of sheer emotion with him, in an ecstatic orgy of spirit in which coherent words only serve to obscure rather than to clarify the message of a personal salvation through Jesus. This kind of worship is unquestionably a product of the Black experience, but totally unrelated to the Black Liberation Struggle. Because it diverts the Black man's attention from present ills and serves as an emotional safety valve, it is not merely irrelevant it is counterrevolutionary.

In light of our collective disunity, it is necessary that we perceive, interpret and utilize the Bible as a *de-fragmentizing* tool. The Black man's deity must be sensitive of and cater to the needs of a displaced, pre-enslaved and exploited people. Perhaps the Bible, as it relates to Black relevance, should be more closely examined. Whom amongst its characters (including Jesus) was ever denied basic human and civil rights because of the color of their skin? Was Jesus, or the lineage, from which he came, ever kidnapped from their homeland and forced to speak their conqueror's language? Was Jesus forced to convert into his conqueror's religion and culture? Did he go by a name given to him by his slave master? Which biblical characters were ever conditioned to hate their skin color, noses, lips and hair texture? What people in the Bible were presented with an image of a savior that looked like their oppressor? These are the things that Black people all over the world have experienced.

If a drug addict is in recovery and seeks advice on how to overcome his addiction, who is better qualified to help him? Would it be someone who has experience in beating addiction or one who has never used drugs?

African Americans are part of an African heritage of people that have been scattered. We are part of the Black Diaspora. In the entire world, there are no predominately Black countries that are in complete control of their wealth generating resources! There is not much political, economic or cultural unity among Black people of various countries. Many of these predominately Black countries have converted to Christianity.

Jesus (or any other deity whom we worship) must be

made relevant to our specific circumstances. Our preachers must extract the information within the lives of various religious prophets and edify us with certain aspects of their stories that are relevant to Black liberation.

Although the story of Jesus is humanitarian in scope, Blacks cannot psychologically afford to have a one-size-fits-all approach to the way we interpret or utilize the information contained within the story of Jesus. We have to have religion with relevance and rituals with reason.

The church must also connect itself to the events that take place outside it. It must make relevant every significant event that affects the Black race. We have to take an all inclusive approach to spirituality. For example, the church must find ways to effectively protest when a Black shoots another Black to death, in exactly the same manner as we would have if a White police officer had done the killing. We should bring attention to it, protest it, and refuse to accept it, regardless of how common its occurrence.

Whenever White police officers shoot and kill Black males, many Black clergy and community leaders either ignore or kick a major fuss about it. We should become outraged whenever this happens, but we should be equally outraged when Black males kill *each other*. The main reason Blacks become more alarmed when White cops kill Black men is because of the history of White authority toward us in this country. We justifiably feel that when Whites murder our young Black males it is an indication or prelude of things to come. Fear motivates this kind of thinking and is precisely the same rationale Whites use whenever Blacks commit crimes against them. Blacks, however, do not have a history of killing Whites, therefore, their fear is often unwarranted. The main thing Whites fear is a payback for what was once done to Blacks. What Whites subconsciously fear is what Malcolm X referred to as the "chickens coming home to roost." Blacks send a dysfunctional message to the world when we "permit" each other to viciously murder one another but loudly protest when a White person does the same thing.

In light of what is happening to our young Black males, the church must take a leadership stand and demand we resolve these serious issues facing our people. Individual salvation must be coupled with a concern for our collective salvation. We are dying from self-inflicted wounds and not just from outer forces, such as racism and genocide.

We need to interact with the church in a more business-like manner. We attend church faithfully, in droves. The difference between a productive race of people and an unproductive one is what they do with their time. We spend too much time in church utilizing it like an emotional factory where we manufacture non-productivity.

Jews attend synagogues and address issues concerning

Jews. It is natural for a rabbi to address matters pertaining to the Jewish community. This is true of many groups. The Black preacher, on the other hand, seems more interested in starting emotional frenzies, which too often determines the success of his sermon. Every time we co-sign and emotionally react to the simple and repetitive remarks of a preacher, we pour gasoline on his fire (ego). This encourages them to keep appealing to our senses and not our sense.

In a symbolic way, the next time we attend church we should be like batters in a baseball game. We should not swing (testify) at every ball the preacher throws us. We need to make sure he throws us strikes. In other words, we should demand that we get on base and score (learn something relevant, practical and applicable). We may just have it backwards. We may be better served if we preach in Sunday school and teach at Sunday service.

6 *Beyond The Literal*

There is no phrase without a double meaning.
– Kenyan Proverb

I have heard many preachers proclaim that "God doesn't change, but His methods do." They back that statement by informing us that if God's methods had not changed, we would still be sacrificing animals. If then, God's methods change, and God is within us and is an example to us, then our methods (biblical interpretations) should also change. Black sermons have to become more provocative, intellectually stimulating and metaphoric. Preachers must teach the people how to dive below the surface of things. One way for preachers to accomplish this is by placing more emphasis on teaching the house than on rocking the house. They must first educate themselves by being open to other ideas from ancient cultures, noteworthy scholars and notable educators.

One of the best ways to transcend the traps of tradition is by moving beyond the realm of literal interpretation and understanding that there are deeper metaphoric and symbolic meanings to many biblical scriptures. For instance, when we hear of prophets or biblical characters going to "mountaintops," we must know that there has to be a deeper and more symbolic meaning to this phrase. We must take into account the altitude of these various mountains, and the climactic changes one would naturally encounter the higher one climbs.

Mount Sinai is estimated by some biblical scholars to be over eight thousand feet high. Going to the mountaintop means elevating to a higher state of consciousness or rising to a higher level of thought.

Another example is found in the biblical story of Jonah where he finds himself inside the belly of a whale. Let's take into account the fact that a whale cannot swallow anything larger than a grapefruit. One may interpret this to mean that we sometimes get ourselves into things so big that it becomes difficult to get out. We are sometimes in places or involved in things where we do not belong. A whale is used to tell the story because it is the largest animal in the world. Some biblical scholars see the story of Jonah as a vision that symbolizes trouble. The biblical story about the wall of Jericho may symbolically represent the "walls" or obstacles we face in life.

Noah, is a biblical character who built an ark and allegedly loaded two of *every living thing* onto it. He was preparing for the coming of a new world and needed a male and female of each creature, so they could reproduce in this new world. How can this story be taken literally? There are over nine thousand different species of birds, and one million species of insects and creatures that to this day have yet to be discovered. And what about amoeba, protozoan, and other single celled organisms that are too small to be seen? Was Noah a biologist? How was he able to distinguish between a male and a female gnat? There are insects that live only a day; how could they survive for weeks inside an ark?

Many biblical passages such as these contain symbolic meanings. Literal interpretations confuse and keep us in biblical training wheels. This may apply to all fundamentalist reading of the scripture.

One of the reasons so much of the Bible is written in the tone of the supernatural is because the stories were written during a time when people read aloud.The books of the Bible were designed to be *heard*. Many people in antiquity did not own Bibles and could not read. Bibles had not yet come into an era of mass distribution. People learned by listening to the stories read to them. This is why the Bible and the stories within it are written so poetically.

Poetry is dramatic and uses symbolism and metaphor to create vivid pictures of the stories being told. Martin Luther King Jr., for example, said that he had been to "the mountaintop and looked over." We know that the great Dr. King did not physically climb a mountain. He was a great orator and found it necessary to use the symbolism of a mountain to illustrate the magnitude of the Civil Rights Movement.

Hardly any of us talk literally all the time. We say things such as "It's raining cats and dogs"; "That person gets under my skin"; "We had a ball last night"; or "That party was off the hook," etc. We use symbolism everyday. We also routinely use metaphors like "time is money" or "men are dogs." Why then are we taught to interpret the Bible literally, especially when it was written during a time when it was fashionable to use dramatic speech?

When preachers teach a literal interpretation of the Bible, it does nothing to stimulate our powers of cognitive reasoning. Our literal beliefs are the foundations of our collective gullibility. It is unfortunate Blacks have been and still are being taught to believe, literally, that a man parted an entire sea and closed it with his outstretched arms. We are taught to believe that a bush can be on fire without it being consumed; a multitude of people were fed with two fish; a boy slew a giant; and a giant whale spit a man onto dry land.

These beautiful and allegorical stories (which are adaptations of many other ancient belief systems) are metaphoric and symbolic in meaning. Blacks are the elders of the earth and the founders of many of our religious belief systems. That may be why we are so susceptible to being spellbound by them.

Certainly we are not the only people who believe in literal interpretations, but where we find other groups believing their spiritual systems in the literal sense, these beliefs are parlayed into a formula for success. Their beliefs are very old and firmly rooted into the fabric of their culture. Black people in America (even though there is much evidence of our pre-Columbus presence), and so many other parts of the world, are a people who are operating on soils not native to us, speaking our conqueror's language, and have been taught other ways of interpreting spirituality. We are, essentially, a hybrid culture. The way in which our White conquerors taught enslaved Blacks to interpret the Bible was a calculated and designed plan to keep them docile. If we had been taught a less literal interpretation of the Bible, it may have liberated and broadened our thinking and also stimulated our ability to use the powers of cognitive reasoning. The intentions, however, of the slave master was not to liberate Black people but keep them sensationalized and grounded in the soil of supernaturalism, instead of the fertile soil of good reason and logic. We are simply playing the religious hand we were dealt.

When the world sees our love of the Bible and our literal interpretations on religion, we are seen wearing our gullibility on our sleeves. Blacks are one of, if not, the most exploited people on earth. It is relatively easy to sell "swamp land" to a people who have a literal outlook on spirituality. It is easy to see why designer clothing, car (and car rim) and gym shoe manufacturers are able to exploit us in such a fashion. We accept too many things at face value. It is high time for a change in our thought processes. We as a whole do not possess the love of intelligence needed to be productive. We are living like the children of the world, instead of the mothers and fathers. Preachers have to pay more attention to the long-term, collective consequences of their short-term, individual church sermons.

Dr. Rocco A. Errico, author of the book *Let There be Light, The Seven Keys*, says that much of the confusion in the Bible is due to a lack of understanding of Aramaic language (original language of the Bible), culture, symbolism, mysticism, psychology, idioms and amplification or exaggeration. In the book, Dr. Errico presents a broader understanding of scripture, "without the restrictions of literal explanations."

Excessive literal interpretations of biblical scripture are expressed in our personifications of God. The literal interpretation within the story of creation, according to Lloyd Graham, author of *Deceptions and Myths of the Bible*, is a "kindergarten account of cosmic phenomena."

The story of creation, found within the first few chapters of Genesis, is where we begin to assign God human attributes.

"And God said, Let there be light: and there was light" (Genesis 1:3). We implicitly ascribe vocal chords (a voice) to God. Who was there to hear what God said and write down His words? How is it that humans instantly developed a language with grammar, phonetics and vocabulary, already established? "And God called the dry *land* Earth; and the gathering together of the waters called he Seas: and God saw that *it was* good"(Genesis 1:10). This creation story is an adaptation of Egyptian Creation Myths as found in *The Book of the Dead* by E.A. Wallis Budge. Hebrew scribes, however, replaced the polytheistic Egyptian gods with a montheistic god.

Furthermore, who is actually capable of interpreting how God felt? This may be very uncomfortable for many Black Christians, but when we have sat in a mental place for a long time it is naturally going to cause some discomfort when we begin to mentally change positions.

Humans see God in an anthropocentric way. In other words, we use ourselves as measuring sticks to describe God. Whenever we view God as a personality rather than a principle, we allow Him to be judged and subjected to the same character scrutiny as anyone else with a personality. We open up the possibility for Him to be questioned based on His perceived attention toward some and His neglect toward others. When we view God as a personality, we place Him on a human level whose existence is one of fallibility.

I once witnessed a woman who upon passing her vehicle inspection, proceeded to shout, praise and thank God. The woman's joy is puzzling when we consider the fact that there are over six billion people in the world. Nearly half of the world's inhabitants earn less than a dollar a day. There are roughly thirty thousand children who die everyday from starvation and disease. Hundreds of thousands of people across the globe (especially in Africa) are afflicted with the A.I.D.S. virus, and there are civil wars in places all over the world.

When we take all of these horrible things into account, what makes us think that God would give a hoot about this woman's car passing its inspection? Would not a God with a *personality* be concerned with more pressing issues facing many of His other children? This by no means is an atheistic remark. These questions are presented here only to illustrate the point that there is a need for deeper, more objective thinking with regard to our concepts of spirituality. What is also important to mention is that prior to the inspection, the woman's car was on course to fail. The inspector went beyond his job description, connecting vacuum hoses which he noticed detached. He also inflated the tires and secured a loose spark plug wire. Ironically, upon leaving the inspection center, the woman began repeating "God is good."

Never once did she give the *inspector* credit. This is typical amongst churchgoers trained to deprecate all that is of man. When good things happen in our lives we often undermine and discredit the ***human*** contribution. "*You* are good" would have been a more appropriate remark from the woman, since it was the inspector that made it possible for her car to pass inspection. The good we attribute to God is the good (God) within us.

The church is largely responsible for our self-deprecating attitudes. The literal way we are taught to interpret the Bible has a lot to do with how we perceive ourselves. When we personify God and adhere to biblical stories colored in supernaturalism, everything natural pales in comparison — including ourselves.

Waiting and Hoping

7

What one hopes for is always better than what one has.
– Ethiopian Proverb

When we measure the psychological impact of the sermonic vocabulary within the church and its affect on the Black psyche, perhaps the church's greatest and most harmful effect is that it has imbued Black people with a spirit of *waiting*. It seems that Blacks are forever waiting for something. We have been conditioned, theologically, to wait for everything. Because we have been conditioned to wait, it has diverted our attention from the social flames that are burning at the moment. It also has deadened our sense of self-accountability.

We have been historically and helplessly waiting for the Lord, waiting for the "Kingdom of Heaven," waiting for the welfare check, waiting to hit the lottery, waiting for the government and waiting for others to do for us what we should be doing for ourselves. We even wait for Democrats to take control of the White House, not realizing we are often more impacted by what is in our local communities and our homes rather than what is happening in city hall or Washington, D.C. When we idly wait and witness people of other nationalities opening businesses in our neighborhoods, it is not necessarily because of whom these people voted to serve in Washington or even in their own city or county. These groups, at some point, made conscious decisions to pool their resources and do business in Black communities.

There are many reasons why various groups nationwide, consistently take advantage of an African American market of consumers. One reason may be that Blacks are blinded by a church-induced fog of waiting. Waiting is not a virtue—patience is. Waiting is tied to wishing. Patience is actively doing something in a systematic way, while exercising the discipline to postpone immediate gratification in order to attain future rewards. Is it all just a coincidence that Black preachers notoriously preach a gospel of waiting, and Blacks are in a dependent and economically fragmented state? It really says something about a people who are inordinately more inclined to consume than to produce.

African Americans, for instance, generate more money from beauty and hair care products than from just about anything else. How is it that other groups, especially Asians, dominate a large percentage of the Black hair care and beauty supply industry when that is one of our biggest moneymakers?

That is the same as Blacks going to Asia and selling rice.

Black preachers are always telling us that our blessings are on the way. A year or two in the future they will still be telling us that "tomorrow" we will be receiving a blessing. When preachers consistently tell us our blessings are on the way (in the future), the illusion is created that we are not blessed at the moment—today. In addition to passing the bowls around to collect money, Black churches need to pass out copies of *National Geographic Magazine*, so we can see just how blessed we truly are. Black people in Sub Sahara Africa and many other parts of the world have been engaged in civil wars for decades and have lost millions of lives due to starvation, disease and war. In Haiti, Blacks have been in political and economic turmoil for many years. Our problems here in America are miniscule compared to most people of color in the world. "Your blessings are on the way" sounds ridiculous when we put our situations into proper perspectives. Only a fool is thirsty in the midst of water.

We also need to rethink our views concerning hope. The slogan "Keep Hope Alive" also needs to be placed in perspective. Hope is a close cousin of wait. According to Webster's New World Dictionary, hope is defined as *a feeling that what is wanted will happen; desire accompanied by expectation.* While enslaved, we hoped to be free one day, and we were eventually "freed." But it was not hope that freed us. It helped to ease the pain of suffering, but it is not tangible; only a *feeling* that what is wanted will happen.

As our needs are met, our goals must change. Our methods must change also, and the traditional styles of preaching will benefit from such a change. Hope is necessary, but it works best when it is all we have. Blacks have so many more resources that can help empower them. We need to combine our beliefs with courses of action. We need a gospel of action, and a gospel that reflects and brings out the intelligence, productivity and global vision in our people that has been largely repressed by the church. Hoping and waiting are best applied in the appropriate situations.

Because of the tormenting experience of slavery, Blacks had little choice but to construct mountains of hope to counteract their feelings of powerlessness. Without the hope of a Messiah returning to earth to free them from bondage, the experience of slavery would have been immeasurably worse. As a consequence, Blacks have evolved into a race of people who are extremely reliant, trusting and dependent upon the future return of Jesus, to the extent that we are delinquent in relying, trusting and depending on the very people whom we live amongst everyday. We are famous for saying, "Jesus will take care of me," "Jesus will make a way," and "Jesus will provide all of my needs."

It is vital to our growth and progress that we also—here

on earth—rely, trust and depend on one another. We are like beautiful Black birds that are unable to fly because we are wrapped too tightly in the ribbons of hope and wait. At the same time, we are sitting on eggs labeled "heaven," while the moment of now passes us by.

An African proverb states: "What is near is dear." This is not a debate on whether or not Jesus is "coming back." The point is to have balance in our lives. Extremism in any form is counterproductive. Waiting and hoping are a big part of the Black theosophical landscape. Blacks are among the most Jesus-praising people on earth, yet amongst the most fragmented and economically dependent. There is a very real correlation between our high praising and low productivity.

Let us assume that Black people were not hoping and waiting for a better day and did not have such high hopes and expectations of a Messiah returning to earth to escort them to Paradise. Wouldn't it then be reasonable to assume that as a consequence, more energy would be diverted to the present? We would have no other option than to deal with the moment. There would be no more rationalizing our privation because the only ones we would expect to change our situations would be ourselves. We would not be able to leave ourselves an out. We would be forced to walk without our mental crutches. Hope is like water; it is good for you, but too much of it will drown you.

8 The Impact of Images

One falsehood spoils a thousand truths.
– Ashanti Proverb

One critical aspect of the Black church that has also been incredibly detrimental to the Black psyche is that many Black churches still have Caucasian images of "Jesus" plastered on their walls or stained into their windows.The great number of Black folks who do not see this as a psychological impediment or consider it an insignificant and harmless gesture, do not understand the real impact images and symbols have on the human brain.They are ignorant of the laws of cause and effect.They are also ignorant to the historical events that have led Blacks to worship and accept images of a Messiah that does not reflect themselves.

One afternoon, I walked into a computer sales and service shop owned by an African man from Nigeria. I instantly noticed two calendars that had pictures of a white image of Jesus. The calendars were very noticeable, so I politely questioned the man (whom I had known for a while) about them and offered to buy some that I thought would be more appropriate for him and the vast majority of his Black customers. He saw absolutely nothing wrong or inappropriate about the calendars and predictably played the colorblind card.

This experience only reinforced how deeply Blacks all over the world have been brainwashed. To see a beautiful dark brother from the Motherland consider it perfectly normal to have not one, but two pictures of a pale white Jesus hanging on his wall, is a reminder of how far removed we are from our proper mindsets.

When Black eyes see Jesus as a White man, the brain's computer logic naturally associates God, the Father, as being White. Have you ever seen a White church with an image of a Black Jesus hanging on their walls or stained into their windows? To project an image of a Messiah that does not look like you is completely unnatural.

An icon of a White Jesus in a Black church is one of the most blatant vestiges of an enslaved mentality that remains within our psyche. Without vision, the people will perish, and unless we visualize ourselves as God-like, we will eventually cease to exist. Churchgoers will claim that color doesn't matter, and Jesus is not partial to any particular race of people. If color is unimportant, then why is he classically portrayed as White? Why do all of the popular and major magazines project Jesus as White? Are they coming from a *historical* perspective or a conquerors? There is a point in time where perception merges with reality, and our White conquerors had very specific reasons why they exposed or concealed certain things to us, their captives. Michael Angelo, summoned by Pope Julius II to do so, painted one of the first classical pictures of a White Jesus.

When the image of a Caucasian Jesus began to spread around the globe, it traveled with a lot of company, mostly conquerors, colonists, enslavers, missionaries and explorers (invaders). No one, of course, would have ever claimed to have seen God, so creating a natural image of His Son as White was expedient for the White conquerors and missionaries whose objective was to physically and mentally enslave Black people. Converting Blacks to Christianity essentially meant converting them into the White value system.

When a little Black boy or girl visualizes a White Messiah upon closing their eyes and praying, it automatically induces a natural brain response that registers a perception of White supremacy and Black inferiority. A psychologically harmful perception has been created and it becomes stronger than reality.

Numerous books on the market expound on the process, necessity and implementation of European imagery and symbolism throughout the continent of Africa. Blacks with homes, businesses and home churches containing images of Jesus not reflective of them, are doing themselves as well as their children a psychological disservice that will negatively manifest itself in some capacity. What we as Blacks consider harmless, other groups see as sick and strange. A Black picture of Jesus in a White church almost seems impossible, yet White images of Jesus in Black churches are common, and accepted all over the world.

Illustration 2

Illustration 3

Illustration 4

Magazine covers such as the ones in illustrations 2, 3 and 4, help to keep people of color in psychological subordination. Also, movies like the *Ten Commandments*, *King of Kings*, and Mel Gibson's *The Passion of the Christ* are movies based on non-verifiable incidents. These types of films vainly and irresponsibly omit the non-white presence in stories and events associated with divine matters (God). *The Passion of the Christ*, like the church, plays upon the people's emotions.

The movie was an over-the-top, made for Hollywood, sensationalizing, literal and exaggerated King James account of the story of Jesus. Mel Gibson is out of his league, not only because he lacks an interpretive understanding of the Aramaic language, but because he is ignorant to Near Eastern culture, symbolism, idioms, psychology and mysticism. If, in fact, Mr. Gibson were knowledgeable concerning these critical elements to understanding the Bible, the movie would have been far less dramatic, controversial and entertaining. We would have seen a normal human story.

By excluding the presence of people of color, *The Passion of the Christ* is just a continuation in a long line of Hollywood Bible movies that disregard them in stories involving godly matters. They are portrayals depicted from the producer's point of view, and whoever controls the images, controls the definitions as well. In the movies, the cowboys beat the "Indians" because they produce the movies.

Speaking of images, I once owned a bookstore in Cincinnati, Ohio, specializing in books relating to Black topics. One afternoon, a young Caucasian boy around the age of eleven or twelve visited the store. He browsed over the children's book section and noticed a few spiritual books that depicted various biblical characters as being Black. This puzzled the young lad because his current orientation had not prepared him for such a cultural shock. He laughed and informed me that there were no Black prophets in the Bible. I smiled and told him there were indeed. He ran out of the store very excited.

The next day, he entered the store with his father, who did not appear to be a happy camper. The father proceeded to admonish me for telling his son such a "terrible lie." I asked the father this question: "If I had told your son there were no Black prophets but that the devil was indeed Black, would you have come to admonish me then?" The father was absolutely speechless and never attempted to answer my question.

There are many images in our society that we deem appropriate or inappropriate. One thing is for certain, there is no other racial group that has had quite the psychological experience of Blacks. Whether it is rationalizing our privation or displaying a picture of a Caucasian Jesus, we must reevaluate many aspects of our thinking as it relates to spirituality.

9 Economic Fragmentation

When spider webs unite, they can tie up a lion.
- Ethiopian Proverb

There is an abundance of preachers who are the sons of former preachers, who perhaps are the sons of former preachers. If a preacher is "called" by God to preach the gospel, then isn't it ironic that so many are "called" from the same address?

Being a head pastor of a church, for the most part, is a very financially lucrative business. Preachers who were raised in a church environment and had family members who were preachers, find an easy transition into the profession. They are very comfortable with the business of the church and understand its inner workings, and what it takes to keep the dollars flowing. It is not necessarily *what* you know, but *whom* you know. It is not who calls you, but whom you call.

Church is big business and every large business has its share of people trying, by any means necessary, to advance within its ranks. Like other major businesses, it has its share of nepotism, backstabbing, string pulling and brownnosing. Obtaining a license to preach and being called by God are two entirely different things. There can be a thin line between prophets and pretenders.

During the civil rights era, the church was a central meeting place for Black national, political and social agendas. It was a place to strategize, a place of refuge and the primary headquarters of the Black community. The role of the church has changed dramatically over the years in terms of its political significance and its role relative to Black causes. As Blacks become more politically diverse, so do our meeting places. The church is no longer the "oval office" for Black people that it once was. It has essentially shifted from its grassroots feed-the-sheep role of the past. It still feeds the sheep to a degree, but they are in positions to do much more.

Today's churches have become preoccupied with growing in size and generating national and international television audiences. Many churches seem to be more concerned with gaining exposure around the country than with having a local agenda. It seems as though the ma & pa churches are a dying breed. Black churches now operate like big business.

In the Atlanta metro area, for example, there are Black churches with memberships exceeding twenty thousand. Now just imagine if 20,000 people tithed only ten dollars (a conservative estimate) a week. That is an incredible total of $200,000 every Sunday and ten million dollars a year—just from one congregation. An intelligent congregation would make it their financial business to know how the church spends their money. The people have the right to hold these churches accountable for their money and demand that they do something for the community and not just build additions to the church.

The Black church, more so than any other Black institution, is in the greatest possible position to make an economic impact on the Black population. But that cannot happen with so many churches existing as separate and private empires. Yes, there are many churches that utilize the tithe money more efficiently than others, providing day care centers, recreational facilities, tutoring, mentoring programs and many other activities. Black churches, in general, have large followings and are in positions to make significant changes, but more has to be expected. W.E.B. Dubois once said, "Economic cooperation among Negroes must begin with the church group."

When people are handing out significant percentages of their already tight budgets, they should expect more. In the Charlotte, North Carolina. area, twenty-five Black churches united to ask banks for affordable banking services and better treatment for their members. In other cases, Jesse Jackson has been among a number of Black persons in leadership positions who have been aiming to shed light on the economically fragmented state of Black America. Jackson, in particular, has promoted the concept of "mission-based investing" to church leaders. He stated that Blacks "must be brought into the age of economic enlightenment." "And church," he said, "must lead the way."

Salem Baptist Church, one of Chicago's largest Black churches, is a 1,700 member flagship church for the Rainbow/PUSH One Thousand Churches Connected economic literacy program. This program helps other churches start financial ministries. There are more than 100 investment clubs that have been formed within Salem Baptist Church. Bonita Parker, director of One Thousand Churches Connected, says that it is "crucial for black churches to take on the role of providing financial stewardship." Parker further added that "many of us are not taught the science of capital and money matters at home, school or work, and the church community setting is an excellent environment to begin the learning and economic empowering process with others you know."

Big Miller Grove Church in Lithonia, Georgia, created an investment club that helps to build its member's stock portfolios. Mt. Carmel Missionary Baptist Church, in Norfolk, Virginia, has a jar filled with ripped up credit cards sitting on the pulpit. Bishop C. Vernie Russell Jr., leads the congregation in a "debt liquidation revival." These churches must be applauded for bringing our economic issues to the forefront.

Many of the more well-known preachers generate incredible amounts of money. They live a life that exudes material excess. How can we make justifications for this when many of us only see our pastors once or twice a week. When we do attend service, we are far too often served a big percentage of re-heated rhetoric? Adding to insult, many renowned preachers are completely inaccessible to their members. They are among the new celebrity breed of untouchables. The inaccessibility of today's new age Black preacher is striking. It reminds me of a verse in a song by the great Bob Marley that says, "How many rivers do we have to cross before we can talk to the boss."

There are no direct pipelines leading to today's big shot preachers. There are voice prompts and long lists of soldiers to go through before we can even think about contacting the commander-in-chief. Many are lucky to get even a handshake from their pastors.

Congregants are sometimes disheartened by the fact that their preachers do not give them the attention they deserve and, in many cases, may not know their names. Pastors usually claim it is not about them anyway, it is about God. They insist that the focus should be on the word of God, and not on them as individuals. Ministering from a distance may be somewhat effective, but a sense of unity, community and intimacy is lost. When sheep can reach out and touch their shepherds, it gives the sheep their sense of belonging.

Black churches must be careful not to outgrow their effectiveness. Bigger is not always better and, in some cases, is worse. At least the Black preachers of the past had time for us. They knew us by name, visited us when we were sick, ate dinner with us and eulogized our family's funerals. They sometimes needed our help from time to time. The once humble Black church has now entered into a stage of extreme commercialism.

Many church supporters of these lofty preachers justify their preacher's inaccessibility. They agree that it would be impossible to know and administer to hundreds or thousands of people. But rest assured, big-time celebrities who donate or tithe large amounts of money to these lofty churches, have direct pipelines to their big-time preachers. Essentially, the more money, celebrity status and power one has, the more "touchable" the pastor becomes. We are consistently seeing our upper echelon preachers posing in the spotlight with other celebrities.

Keep in mind that these corporate churches with "Fortune 500" preachers were deliberately marketed to be huge. They do not have their current memberships because they are necessarily so much better preachers than those of smaller churches.

It is because they have invested more advertising dollars. High dollar preachers have marketed their "product" on billboards, cassettes, CDs, cable TV, commercials, books, magazines, newspapers, internet and radio. They would not invest large sums of money toward marketing, if they were not expecting huge returns.

Whenever we have a corporate preacher with an international ministry, it is likely that a portion of our tithe dollars go toward advertising, marketing and the general expenses associated with reaching people in foreign countries. Television via satellite is very costly, and our tithe dollars are sometimes spent on things that do not concern or affect us directly. Why should any of our money go abroad? Although it is important for us to think globally, we still live locally. We are naturally opposed to the government using our tax dollars to "assist" people in foreign countries, especially since many of us are homeless, poor and deprived in this country. International ministries operate under the guise of "saving the world," but a greater outreach can sometimes lessen the "in-reach."

Ideas, concepts and innovative thinking change the world. Preaching to the world and promoting religious points of view connotes an act of control and power. Throughout history, the promulgation of religious ideas has been the spark plug that has ignited many battles. There have been more people killed in the name of religion than all of the secular wars combined.

Christianity is the most popular religion in the world, and primarily because it has been promoted the most. During the times of Constantine and the Great Roman Empire, Christianity was declared the official religion, and those who opposed this declaration placed their lives in danger.

The world needs a change. Religion may be able to provide positive results in one's life, but it is just *one* source. Black pastors preach the "Word of God" because they have been taught that it is the official and authentic word. It is the idea we have been presented with. If Christianity is the most popular religion in the world and the King James Version is the authentic word of God, then why isn't the world better? Why do people of color always seem to get the short end of the stick?

Getting back to the business of the church, it is disturbing to see the financial disparity between preachers and their congregations. Many preachers rationalize their material gluttony by saying that it's all a "blessing from God." They say, "God wants us to have money and nice things" and that "Jesus wasn't poor." A true man of God, of course, needs to be compensated for his time and effort, but to what extent? The ostentation of a preacher sends messages to his congregation. What type of message does it send to them when they see their preacher "bling, blinging?" Is the preacher implying that when we are truly one of God's representatives, this is how we'll be blessed?

There are too many extravagant preachers and upscale Black churches across the country. Black preachers can be perhaps the most ostentatious among us, and like sheep, we follow our shepherds. In all fairness, there are good Black preachers, who are productive businesspersons, making gallant efforts to unite with other financially capable businesses and clergy to enhance the community in many aspects. They are the exceptions to the majority of Black preachers. These outstanding preachers work tirelessly to be creative in their sermons as well as their business ventures. They utilize the tithe money in ways that are beneficial to the people. We must applaud them for their efforts and use them for a model.

Preachers, however, have to understand that it is sometimes hard for many congregants to give ten percent of what they barely have in the first place. We must be practical and fervent in our financial matters. We tithe ten percent and are told to expect a blessing in return. Our bill collectors do not expect anything but a check around the first of the month. Although we are children of God, we also live in a capitalistic system, and one of the first laws of financial freedom is to *pay yourself first.* When we do this we will be paying a child of God. There are many churches that keep track of our tithe dollars and make no bones about approaching us if they think we have not been tithing enough. It is sad to think we can actually be put out of church or pressured into leaving, if we are not forking out enough money. Many churches even collect W2 Forms from their members!

I have heard so many people say that the money is not for the preacher but for God. Firstly, there are million dollar churches that are completely paid for, yet many of the sermons continue to have themes based on *giving*. We often walk out of church commenting on how "they were begging today."

Secondly, if God created the whole world and everything in it without a single penny, why all of a sudden does He need money? Preachers choose to go out and build expensive churches with high tech amenities. They take people for granted, but the people, on the other hand, have made it easy to be taken advantage of. Our historical pattern of commitment and devotion to the church is well documented and easy to exploit. Financial institutions are aware of the dollars generated by Black churches, and they are often more than willing to loan the money to build one. "Build, and they will come" is the belief held by banks and Black preachers. How did a people with such humble beginnings manage to make church into a corporate industry? The "progress" of the church is not, in any way, an indicator of the overall collective progress of Blacks. One thing is sure, there is progress in terms of the money generated in the business of preaching.

The church, of course, is not totally responsible for Black people's economic conditions, but it cannot play a role in economically exploiting the masses in the same manner that any other institution would do. Think about this for a minute. Black people have been tithing generation after generation, yet we do not own the centers where we hold our church conventions and Mega Fests. Where are our own schools, hospitals, factories, assembly plants, hotels, airlines, car lines, bus lines, major corporations? The great Marcus Garvey asked these same questions nearly a century ago! It is incredible to think that in 1860, 98% of Blacks in America worked for Whites. In 2001, 98% of Blacks were still working for Whites! What have we done with our money?

Black churches have made billions of dollars, and we have too little across the country to show for it. Why all the preaching? Why aren't we teaching people the principles involved in making our money work for us by recycling it where we live? Black Churches must make Black liberation, economics and empowerment a priority. The bottom-line in the sermons cannot only be about the morality of being good, sitting up straight and being prepared to go to heaven whenever our number is called. Where is our economic independence and collective power? In almost every Black community you see a Black church owned by Blacks, but nearby there is a convenience store owned by non-Blacks. There is no logical explanation for this when we take into account the enormous amount of money generated annually by Black churches across the country. We patronize these stores (owned by non-Blacks) following church service, looking, smelling and feeling good. Far too often, however, the merchants barely speak to us. They rarely say thanks and then watch us like hawks while we shop.

We have been disillusioned with the idea that somebody is going to take care of us. A prosperous church over here, a prosperous church over there and an economically deprived community in the middle, makes no sense at all. If we consider the church to be the backbone of the community, it is about time it started showing some.

Many preachers have biblical-sized egos. A lot of them are totally addicted to the power that comes with being a minister, and it is very easy to see why. Church members flirt with them, ask them for prayer, suck up to them and virtually agree with everything they say. We must remember that the earliest Black preachers (as such) emerged on plantations. For an ex-slave to claim to be a representative of God was a monumental notion. When they had knowledge about a savior "introduced" to them by their masters, they were often considered the cream of the crop. Preaching, then and now, is considered to be among the most prestigious of all occupations.

Preachers with private empires must at some point put their egos and material aspirations aside; meet with other preachers, community citizens and leaders; examine and evaluate the collective economic predicament of Blacks; and decide on a concrete plan of action that will make positive economic impacts on our communities.

Posturing and politicking runs rampant among Black clergy and businessmen. We are in desperate need of jobs and must commit ourselves to creating them. We need to restore our communities, help to improve our quality of living and commit ourselves to achieving prosperity on all levels. Money can greatly help to dissolve some of our societal problems. With all of the money Black churches have generated over the last twenty years, it is conceivable that we could have hired our own personal drug task forces in several major cities to help get drugs off our streets.

The Black Muslims are among the bravest and most practical among us. They have done a great deal to rid our streets of filth. Many of them do not necessarily adhere to the gospel of Jesus, yet they are known to get out in the trenches in the midst of dangerous drug dealers. They carry no weapons, except those of love and dignity. They are demonstrating practicality and sacrificing themselves for the good of the whole.

They are an example of religion with relevance. They understand that it is our responsibility, despite the fact that "we don't own the planes that bring drugs into the country" or the fact that "we don't manufacture any guns." We cannot continue to ask others, including the government, to always solve *our* problems, regardless of how they occurred.

This is not a plug or promotion for Islam over other religions. It is simply a beautiful example of pragmatism and utilitarianism at work.

Every time I pass or see an extravagant Black church on television, I think about the Led Zeppelin song *Stairway to Heaven*, which sings about a lady who is trying to buy her way into heaven. Is this why there are so many preachers ferociously competing over having the biggest and fanciest church? They may not admit they're competing, but they are.

The current trend of new-age Black churches is to seat thousands of people and generate cash. There seems to be no spiritual basis for these financial endeavors. There is a new, big-shot Black church popping up somewhere in the country all the time. It doesn't do the community any good to have a new, classy church but keep the same old "southern fried chicken" preaching. What big and new collective gains are we making? What significant sermonic changes are we making that will create more community and cultural empowerment?

We need to build less expensive and more basic structures, and invest the difference into the community, where it makes good sense. Ostentation addiction is preventing this from becoming a reality. Today, Black churches have dome tops, acres of land, traffic police, high-tech security and P.A. systems. Then, during the service, they pass the bowls around and expect us to pay for all of that. With all of the glitter associated with today's Black churches, if we did not know any better, we would think there was really something new going on inside.

10 At the Crossroads

It's a bad child who does not take advice.
- Ashanti Proverb

Because of our past struggles, following the importation of Africans into the "New World," the church has been our emotional nest and safety valve protecting us whenever we need to escape the injustices we encounter in society. The Black church and Black people have, in a sense, grown up together. The church (as such) emerged during slavery and became the most dominant and stable institution we have known.

John S. Mbiti pointed out in his book, *African Religions and Philosophy,* that even prior to the importation of Africans to North America, Blacks were notoriously religious. They were already socialized in their own African traditions.

It is important to keep in mind that the first Black churches made no real distinction between sacred input and secular output. The preachers were often the most educated among us and moonlighted as political leaders and abolitionists. Frederick Douglass, a Black freedom fighter, was a preacher in Rochester, New York. The three largest slave revolts in American history originated from the hands of preachers: Gabriel Prosser, Denmark Vesey and Nat Turner. Black churches served as meeting and hiding places for the Underground Railroad.

Black Methodists organized the first denominations and national associations for Blacks. Richard Allen and Absalom Jones established the Free African Society of Philadelphia. We cannot forget that the establishing of the first Black denominations came as a result of Allen and Jones being kicked out of a White church while they were on their knees praying.

Social and political purposes were driving forces behind our early church founders. Fighting for freedom, human dignity, equal rights and justice were the causes the early and civil rights era churches promoted. Today's Black churches must follow in the early church's footsteps and make getting to heaven *on earth* a priority.

Despite our renowned devotion to the church it is very sad to think that there is not one predominately Black country on earth that is in complete control of their wealth generating resources. Moreover, in this country, where wealth is abundant, it is almost embarrassing to see all the emotional Black revivals taking place, yet we hardly manufacture, produce or trade anything. We must seem very peculiar to the rest of the world.

There is a total disconnection of inspiration and application as it relates to our actions when the church service has ended. We are still leaving church feeling good and uplifted and immediately going to spend our dollars outside of our communities. We continue to heavily patronize establishments that do not have our interests at heart. Many church treasuries receive our Black dollars on Sunday morning and deposit them into White banks on Monday morning. We leave church praising the Lord, yet go right back to our same conditions and foolish behavior.

Collective success and nationwide progress is a slow process, but how long should this take? At this point in our social development, it is very reasonable to think that African Americans should be bigger players in this free enterprise system of capitalism. It is quite possible for Blacks to own major manufacturing plants, hotels, factories, or other major establishments.

Whether we attend church or not, the vast majority of Blacks in the United States are either directly or indirectly influenced by the sermonic indoctrination of the church. We are the collective seed of a central doctrine that has germinated out of the most influential institution on the Black thought process. I am not suggesting we stop attending church, but if we stay in the church, WE MUST GROW and exert our influence on changing its direction. The church should not be viewed exclusively as a place to worship but also as a breeding ground for empowerment. Our religious or spiritual lights must shine so that men may see our good works, not hear our good preaching.

The Japanese people are a prime example of a people who appear to have an understanding that spirituality and practicality are one. Most Japanese adhere to both Shintoism and Buddhism.

American bombs devastated parts of Japan during World War II. The country has since rebounded to become a true heavyweight in the world's economy, and one of the most technologically advanced countries. Japan has one of the highest life expectancies in the world, and virtually everyone can read and write because of its excellent educational system. The Japanese are able to internalize their spiritual teachings and, most importantly, apply them to their everyday life.

The Black church needs to take a thorough inventory of itself. High praising in church and low productivity outside of it is a sign of an institution and a race of people that are misreading what spirituality is supposed to be about. If we worked on saving money as much as we do on saving souls, we would be a race of producers instead of consumers. If we kept the dollar in the Black community as we keep the dollar in the church, we would be major economic players. If we prepared for our future on earth the way we prepare for our future in the hereafter, our children would have a legacy from which to benefit.

> [Martin Luther King observed] There are still too many Negro churches that are absorbed in a future good "over yonder" that they condition their members to adjust to the present evils "over here."

Dr. King also stated:

> This lopsided Reformation theology has often emphasized a purely otherworldly religion, which stresses the utter hopelessness of this world and calls upon the individual to concentrate on preparing his soul for the world to come. By ignoring the need for social reform, religion is divorced from the mainstream of human life.

The Black church must be more than a present day crutch, predicated upon a future reward. If we put out as much application as we take in inspiration, our communities would be more prosperous. If we studied the principles of finance only half as much as we study the Bible, our future on earth would be brighter. If we were as flamboyant with our intelligence as we are with our material possessions, the whole world would benefit. If we were as committed to our collective salvation as we are to our individual salvation, we would be the giants of the earth. If we built businesses as we build churches, we would be in charge of the stock market.

We can do these things and still keep the church, but we must seek heaven in the secular sense. We can no longer afford to attend church with our hearts on our sleeves. We have to see it for what it is. We must choose to use the church to our advantage by making it work for us. The church, among other things, is a tool and a business. It is the most visible example of financial success in our communities. It can be a very useful tool and a very profitable business. Black preachers are in terrific positions to provide us with the information we need to stop the bleeding.

The church holds our people at bay for thousands of hours each week across the nation, therefore, it is in the best position to return us to our proper state of respectability. The church has the people, the resources and the time to make a much greater difference.

We have to see the power our thoughts possess, and we must see our thoughts as creative forces capable of achieving anything. The church needs overhauling and reevaluating. We, also, have to let go of our "my preacher can do no wrong" mentalities so that we can begin to make room for progress. Preachers are men and women who are susceptible to the same positive and negative energies we all encounter. They must make more of an effort to fuse the pulpit with the community. This must be done without working under the pretext of recruiting new members. Preachers must turn their vertical existence onto a horizontal plane with the rest of us. They are fallible human beings and not mystical, supernatural highborn persons with all of the right answers.

We defend our churches and preachers on every account. We are all too quick to point out the many wonderful things our particular church is doing. Do not be disillusioned. Whatever wonderful program or activity our particular church is involved in—we paid for it.

The point is not to necessarily stop attending church but to grow up in the church. Redundant, counterproductive sermons produce gullable and non-productive people. Preachers must provide more than just re-heated, sensationalizing and over-dramatic rhetoric that is irrelevant to Black progress.

We may experience some grief when we move beyond traditional sermonic rhetoric. We may also experience growing pains. This perceived loss or grief we may encounter, is worth the price of the benefits we will gain through the inevitability of change. Many of us have heard the expression *love is letting go*. We have to love ourselves enough to let go of rituals without reason, denominations without investigation, rhetoric without a collective agenda, emotionality without practicality and tradition without progress.

One of the most fundamental lessons that people learn, who are suffering from substance abuse and addiction, is that one cannot continue to do the same things and expect different results. Addicts refer to this behavior as insanity. The church cannot continue to be the same way, do the same things, preach the same messages, while at the same time expecting significant changes in the people. It seems as though we have become addicted to the good feelings that churches induce. We cannot continue to be slaves to tradition and rituals. It is time to let go of our *when the saints go marching in* mentalities.

Eventually, we are going to have to determine whether or not we are collectively benefiting and progressing from our traditional modes of theosophical indoctrination. The Black church must be put on trial and held accountable for what it does and does not do; what it emphasizes and what it ignores. What better time than now to begin the process of evaluating our sacred input and factoring it into our quest toward Black liberation.